The Mystery of Fate:
Common Coincidence or Divine Intervention?

Real Stories ~ Real People

Compiled and Edited by
Arlene Uslander and Brenda Warneka

To my friend, Jill,
I think your
grandparents and my
parents would like to know
we connected.
Good Fate to you
always.
Love,
Arlene

© 2010 by Arlene Uslander and Brenda Warneka
ISBN: 978-0-9819654-2-0

First Edition – Published February 2010
Printed in the U.S.A.

R. J. Buckley Publishing
Queen Creek, AZ

Acknowledgments

To our story contributors, we express our deep appreciation and thanks for your patience, your willingness to answer our seemingly endless questions in our efforts to make sure we had the facts straight, and for your encouragement, support, and loyalty. And, of course, for your wonderful stories. We hope that someday, we can meet and thank each of you in person.

To Stephanie Grossi, a very talented graphic designer, for enthusiastically working with us to come up with a very memorable photo collage for the front cover.

To Hank Wilson, Larry Hicks, and Jacob Herbst, subjects of three of our stories, thank you for graciously giving us your time and making it such a pleasure to interview you. We felt that you each had a compelling story to tell, and with your patient help, we were able to tell it.

To all whom we have mentioned, and to many others—those of you who led us to people who had stories to share; consultants whose advice we sought and received on technical matters, and to friends and family who believed in us and our idea for this book, thank you for helping us "keep the faith" to keep on going with "Fate."

Arlene and Brenda

Note: Quotations with no attribution after them are by the author of the particular story wherein they appear.

About the Editors

When I first got the idea of putting together a collection of stories about fate, I posted an announcement on a writers' website soliciting submissions. I received only one response from a person named Brenda. She wanted to know whether an experience involving her husband would be appropriate for my book. She described the incident; I e-mailed her back, saying that it sounded just like what I was looking for. About a week later, she sent me the story. It was perfect for the anthology. You will see why when you read "Fate on the Fly."

We subsequently started e-mailing back and forth, and got to be what you might call "good e-mail buddies," telling each other about our families, our work, our vacations; the kinds of things most women talk about when they first become acquainted. The fact that we lived in different parts of the country—she in Arizona, I in Illinois—and that our work experience was totally different—she a lawyer and a businesswoman, I a retired elementary school teacher, and freelance editor—didn't seem to get in the way of our e-mail friendship. After all, we are both writers. That is how and why we met on a writers' website.

After corresponding for about a year and a half, we decided it was time to meet. It just so happened that my husband and I, and Brenda and her husband, were going to be in Florida at approximately the same time, so we decided the four of us should meet for a weekend.

My husband and I picked up Brenda and her husband at the hotel where they were staying, which was only a few blocks from the house I had rented for my family. Having exchanged pictures, we easily recognized the other. We greeted each other warmly, introduced our husbands, and from that moment on, it was as though we had been friends all our lives. What made everything even nicer was that our husbands discovered they had so much in common. They both are businessmen, they love to cook, and have a great time browsing through stores, especially Costco and Trader Joe's!

About a year after we met in person, I asked Brenda if she would consider being the co-editor of this book. I thought it would be fun to work together (albeit long distance). Her response was short and (not so) sweet: "NO! NO! NO!" She explained that she was much too busy with work, family, friends and various activities to take on yet another project. Somehow, though, after a lot of cajoling, pleading and *begging,* I was able to convince her. What I didn't realize until after Brenda started working with me is what an outstanding editor she is. So I got much more than I bargained for: a fun co-editor, superb editing skills, and someone to help with the story selection.

The fact that Brenda was the first one (actually the only one) to send a story in response to my announcement on that particular writers' website, and ended up being my co-editor and very good friend, seems to me like kind of a fate story in itself— as though she just happened to be surfing the Internet late one night, at the right place, at the right time, and was interested and curious about my "intriguing fate announcement" (or so I thought it was!). But our meeting on the Internet had even more important implications, as you will find out when you read my story "God Writes Straight Lines in Crooked Letters." Actually, if the truth be known, she saved my life, or at the very least, prolonged it.

What you are about to read are stories we both selected from hundreds that were submitted, and if you notice any typos or misspellings, they are my fault, not Brenda's.

By the way, Brenda's suspenseful and heartwarming story "The Traffic Stop" won first place in the non-fiction category in the prestigious magazine *Arizona Attorney*. When you read the story, you will understand why she won first place!

As for our wonderful contributors, they come from all over the world. Some have also won writing awards; others are sure to win awards, as they are all fine writers. Even more important, they are fine human beings. Be sure to read their bios at the end of their stories.

Arlene Uslander, Co-Editor

About the Photos

The photographs on the cover are as follows, clockwise:

1. Map showing Alexandria, Egypt, where Vicka Markov Surovtsov's story "Miracle in Alexandria" took place.

2. Hank Wilson, the policeman in "The Traffic Stop," in a photograph taken circa 1962, when the story took place.

3. The author of "The Sapphire Ring," Katherine Kimsey, with her husband, JD, and their oldest son, Robert, in 1946.

4. Standard Poodles, BonBon and Maggie, whose story is told in "The Sisters," shown with their owner and the author of the story, Brenda Warneka.

5. A view from New York Harbor of the Twin Towers burning on that infamous day, 9-11, some events of which gave rise to Arlene Uslander's story "Jacob! Jacob! Reborn September 11, 2001."

6. A rosary, a string of beads used in counting prayers by Catholics, which plays a central role in "The Rosary," a story by Ann Wilkes.

7. Dr. Sun Yat-sen (1866-1925), Chinese revolutionary, widely revered in both Mainland China and Taiwan, who played a major role in the life events of author Aimee Lui's grandparents in "The Quake That Made a Marriage."

Cover collage by Stephani Grossi, graphic designer, Stephanie Grossi Designs. - www.stephaniegrossidesign.com

Table of Contents

What is Fate?

Luck of the draw, or meant to be? Our lives are impacted by forces we cannot explain, often changed for reasons we will never totally understand. However, when people are touched by the hand of fate, they know it. Whether fate brings them their heart's desire, or forever closes the door to their dreams, the path that has brought them to that point is clear, and fate's irony is unmistakable.

Thomas Wilson
Writer, musician, philosopher

THE MYSTERY OF FATE:

The Traffic Stop

By Brenda Warneka

What we anticipate seldom occurs; what we least expect generally happens.

Benjamin Disraeli

It was after midnight in late February 1962, and bad weather had kept most drivers in Grosse Pointe Park, Michigan, home for the evening. Bone-chilling sleet, followed by snow, had made for icy, slushy roads in the small Detroit suburb.

The old, shiny green Packard moving east on Jefferson Avenue caught Patrolman Hank Wilson's eye for two reasons. First, he loved that line of cars, and this one was really nice with customized rear bubble skirts. Second, the car was too clean for this time of year, with no mud or salt stains. Hank was a policeman who trusted his intuition. Imagining that the car might be going a little too fast for road conditions was reason enough to stop the driver.

Hank maneuvered his police cruiser out of a side street where he had been parked, turned on his siren and gave chase. The Packard swung quickly over to the curb and stopped. Hank got out of his vehicle and approached the car, leaving his partner, Bill Crandall, slouched in the passenger seat, chin on his chest, snoring peacefully. Police protocol required the second officer to be alert to provide assistance in case of trouble, but Hank did not want to disturb Bill.

The driver of the Packard, a man who appeared to be in his early twenties, rolled down his window. He had a bulky wool coat folded across his lap. A young woman, who appeared to be a few years younger than the driver, sat next to him. Hank stood back at an angle from the driver's window, a defensive stance that allowed him to move quickly if a problem arose.

"Good evening," Hank said to the driver. Then, without waiting for a response: "How do you keep your car so clean in this type of weather?"

The driver seemed taken aback with the abruptness of the question. "Oh, me and Bonnie—this is Bonnie," he said, nodding toward the woman beside him. "We just got married. I washed the car for the wedding. We're supposed to be on the expressway on our way to Chicago now, but I took a wrong turn."

In spite of the biting cold of the night air, a warm feeling flooded over Hank. He was only a few years older than the driver, and it had not been that long since he and Mildred were married. He thought of her at home now, undoubtedly fast asleep.

"Let me see your license," Hank said. He was now at the driver's door, bent over a little, looking slightly down at the driver and into the interior of the car.

The man shifted his weight to one side and pulled a wallet out of his back pocket. He removed a driver's license and passed it to Hank through the open window.

Hank shined his flashlight on the document. It was a Michigan license in the name of Bruce Hemelberg, and it had expired a few days earlier.

"Bruce, did you know your license is expired?" Hank asked.

"Yes." The driver flinched at the question. Cold air was pouring in through the car's open window, and he slid his hands beneath the warmth of the coat on his lap.

Then he looked up earnestly into Hank's eyes. "It's only just expired. Bonnie and me are moving to Chicago to live, and times are tough. I didn't want to waste money getting the license renewed here when I'd have to pay for a new one as soon as we hit Chicago."

Hank could relate to that. He had experienced how tight budgets could be for young newlyweds. Every dollar made a difference.

"Let me see your registration," he said.

"It's my mom's car," Bruce explained. He motioned to Bonnie with his head to look in the glove compartment. She pulled out some documents, peered at them in the dim light from the glove box, and passed them over to Bruce to give to the officer. Hank examined the registration first. It was for another car in the name of Norma Hemelberg, but there was a bill of sale to this car, and the license plates belonged to Norma. He handed the paperwork back to Bruce through the open window.

"Got any outstanding tickets?" Hank asked.

"No—no." Bruce shook his head, but Hank detected a note of uncertainty.

"Now you need to be sure, Bruce, because if I check, and you do, I'll have to take you in. You were going a little fast just now, but I'm ready to let you go. If you have any outstanding tickets though, tell me now before it's too late." Police procedure required Hank to check for outstanding warrants once he had stopped a driver, but he was thinking again about what it was like to be newly married and broke.

"No, I ain't got any tickets," the man assured him.

"Wait here," Hank said, and walked back to the police car where he woke up Crandall to radio Hemelberg's information into headquarters. A few minutes later, the radio crackled back the report of an outstanding warrant for running a red light in Detroit. It was not a major warrant, but now the officers had less latitude in how to proceed. Because an arrest was involved, they were required to call a second patrol car to assist in taking Hemelberg to the station.

Hank walked back to the Packard, shaking his head. "I told you to tell me if you had any outstanding tickets, Bruce. Why didn't you tell me you had an outstanding ticket for running a red light? I don't have any choice now that we've checked. We've got to take you in."

"I'm sorry," Bruce gulped. "I forgot about the ticket." In spite of the cold air, beads of perspiration appeared on his forehead, which Hank took to mean he could not post the bail to pay the ticket. The young man was nervously hugging the coat on his lap.

"Look," Hank said, "I'll tell you what I'll do. I'll give you the money to pay the ticket. Based on the citation, the bail should be fifty dollars. I'll give it to Bonnie, and she can post the bail after we get to the station, but I'm going to have to formally arrest you and book you at the jail first."

"Well, that sure is decent of you to give me the money to post bail." Bruce shook his head in disbelief. "Give me your home address, and I'll mail the fifty dollars back to you as soon as I can."

"Mail it to me at the station," Hank told him. He figured he would never see the money again, but he felt good for his small act of charity—somewhat in the nature of a wedding gift to Bruce and Bonnie. "When the other patrol car gets here, you need to follow my car to the station."

As it turned out, when they got to the police station, additional information came to light that showed Bruce Hemelberg had more than an outstanding ticket for running a red light. He was a hold-up man, an alleged killer of a mob runner, and he was wanted by five different law enforcement agencies, including the Michigan State Police. His girlfriend, Bonnie—whom Bruce had met at a Saturday night dance at a mental facility where they were both confined—was his accomplice in crime and the mastermind behind the hold-ups. They had escaped from the institution some time back after Bonnie got them a weekend pass in return for sexual favors she was said to have granted one of the facility's psychiatrists.

The Packard was stolen from a garage where it had been stored for the winter, which accounted for the lack of mud or salt stains, and Bruce admitted during questioning that he and Bonnie had been scouting for an all-night store to rob when he was stopped by Patrolman Hank Wilson. When Hank searched the car after Bruce was booked, he found a loaded shotgun, sawed off at both ends, almost to the size of a pistol, hidden under the heavy wool coat that Bruce had left in the back seat when he got out of the car at the police station.

Hemelberg later admitted at trial that at the time of the traffic stop, he had been driving with the sawed-off shotgun concealed under the coat on his lap. He and Bonnie had agreed, when they realized Hank was pulling them over, to shoot the officer. Bruce had his hand on the trigger underneath the coat, aimed at Hank, while Hank was questioning him.

"I meant to kill him," Bruce testified. "I really meant to kill him. But I couldn't pull the trigger—he was just too nice."

Patrolmen Wilson and Crandall received commendations for their outstanding police work in arresting two dangerous criminals. Bruce Hemelberg was sentenced to Jackson State Prison in Jackson, Michigan, for a term of five to thirty years for his crimes, not including the alleged murder of the mob runner, which the authorities were unable to pin on him due to lack of a body. Bonnie was sentenced to one to five years in the Detroit House of Corrections.

Three days after Bruce's release from the state prison in 1972, he instigated a three-hour siege and shootout at a party store in Hazel Park, Michigan, including taking a twenty-five-year-old woman hostage. He was shot to death by a police marksman. He was twenty-nine. He is buried in Macomb County, Michigan. Bonnie's whereabouts after she was released from the Detroit House of Corrections are unknown.

Hank Wilson, the policeman whom fate had favored because he was "nice," today lives in Scottsdale, Arizona, with his wife, Mildred. He is an executive with a computer software development and licensing company.

Brenda Kimsey Warneka has spent her working life in the world of law and business, including many years in the private practice of law. She mainly writes on legal topics, but also on history, travel and human interest. Her story "The Traffic Stop" won first place in the non-fiction category of the 2008 Creative Arts Competition sponsored by the *Arizona Attorney* magazine. Brenda is married with children and grandchildren. She is a member of the Arizona Press Women and lives in Paradise Valley, Arizona, with her husband Dick.

Journey to Healing

By Andrea Eberly

Fate is the symphony of our choices — but WHO is the director?

Sleepy Time tea is boiling on the stove, and I am about to go to bed, winding down after a long day as the Emergency Medical Services Director for the Island of Guam.

"How did you choose to go into medicine?" you ask.

My thoughts drift back to my conservative high school in Germany. This is the place where I developed my first intense, longing career dreams, but medicine was not one of them. My dreams centered on becoming a circus acrobat. I fantasized about lifting people out of their daily lives with beautiful, artistic stunts. I wanted the audience's imagination to soar with me under the ceiling of the circus tent, temporarily leaving all worries and pains behind.

To my parents' credit, they never made fun of my circus dreams. They did suggest that I visit a career-counseling center to explore alternatives. I followed their advice, and the career counselor suggested that I become, not a circus acrobat, but a physician.

The suggestion left me in a state of turmoil. I felt disappointed that she had not supported my dream, yet I also felt a shy pride and a strange excitement about the thought of becoming a doctor.

As I walked home, however, mounting fears replaced that fleeting pride and excitement about a career in medicine. A doctor? Not a circus acrobat? By the time I arrived home, I had dismissed the career counselor's suggestion. The circus tent seemed to be a much more beautiful place to work than the white, sterile corridors of a hospital.

Also, the memory of my incredibly old, female childhood pediatrician made me feel that a career in medicine would mean giving up my youth, beauty, and feminine qualities. Finally, I simply was critical of the field itself, hesitant because I had heard people complain that modern medicine was no longer a healing profession because it viewed disease in terms of body parts and not patients.

A few months later, my circus dreams were shattered. I found out that I was too old to be accepted into the acrobat school in Scotland upon which I had been counting. It was the only acrobat school that I was aware of, so a lonely post-high school period ensued during which I wondered what I should do with my life.

I agonized over the career counselor's suggestion. Did she know something that I did not know? I finally entered college where, much to my own surprise, I felt compelled to include pre-medical courses in my potpourri of studies that ranged from yoga and gymnastics to film writing and philosophy.

The time came to either apply or not apply to medical school. I decided that it never had been my own idea to study medicine. What would I have become if I had never gone to a career counselor? Certainly not a physician.

I decided against medicine and, instead, pursued a Master's Degree in Cybernetics (the study of the management of complex systems). I enjoyed the cybernetics program very much and would have become a consultant in that field had it not been for another turn of events. One day, during a visit to my doctor, he asked me, "Have you ever thought about studying medicine? You would be a fine doctor." For some reason, it felt as though his question was opening an old wound.

I shared my concerns about medicine with the doctor, and told him that my current career choice was final. I did not tell him about the years I had spent during my undergraduate studies debating and re-debating whether or not I should become a doctor. I also did not let him know that even now, after having chosen another career, something continued to tug at the very core of my being every time I crossed paths with medicine.

During my next appointment, the doctor introduced me to an unusually attractive young lady who happened to be a physician. She was a fascinating woman, very intelligent, and also beautiful and caring. She glowed when describing her job. She was quite different from my old childhood pediatrician who had been my only previous female physician role model. I truly enjoyed my conversation with this young doctor, and I went home with nagging feelings that my preconceived notions about medicine might be false.

When I returned for a follow-up visit, my doctor had an application for medical school in his office. He handed it to me and said, "You do whatever you think is right for you, but this year's deadline for applying to medical school is rapidly approaching. I brought these forms in case you want to give it a try."

After much contemplation, I filled out the forms. Due to financial restrictions, I was only able to complete the application process to one school, the UCLA Medical School. To my surprise, I was accepted. I once again wavered about my ability to be a physician, but before I could again turn my back on medical school, another turn of events occurred.

I had partly financed my graduate studies by being a live-in manager of an apartment house in a low-income area. For years I had successfully juggled the demands of the landlord for punctual rent collection against the complete disinterest of the tenants in paying on a timely basis. But just a few weeks before the beginning of medical school, and with only my Master's thesis left to write, I, for the first time, encountered threats of violence from two tenants while trying to collect rent from them. Faced with an increasingly unsafe living arrangement, and encouraged by UCLA to join their medical school, I decided to move to Los Angeles and write my thesis there, while giving medical school a try.

When I entered medical school, I found my childhood fears about medicine surfacing one more time. This time, however, fate brought a conclusion to the issue. Norman Cousins, a famous journalist and writer who had written a book about the value of humor in the healing process, gave a lecture that I attended during my first few months of medical school. He talked about medicine from a patient's perspective, and about how physicians often tend to the patient's body, but forget the patient's soul. He said one cannot heal without the other. I was on the edge of my chair. Here was a man who was addressing the heart of my concerns about medicine. I asked many questions during the lecture.

Sensing my interest, Mr. Cousins sought me out after class and invited me to lunch. I was deeply honored and spilled out my fears to him that modern medicine might no longer be a healing profession. I confessed my serious doubts about continuing medical school. Finally, he said, "There is a need in the medical field for people with your kind of doubts and questions. What would it take for you to commit?"

I thought for a long time. It wasn't until he finished his lunch that I finally answered. "I used to have this philosophy professor at San Jose State University who really inspired me. If *he* were to tell me that medical school was the right thing for me, then I would finish."

Mr. Cousins nodded. "So, how do you get in touch with your professor?"

Sadly, I told him that this professor had left for Sweden several years before, and I no longer knew his whereabouts. Mr. Cousins said that if I could locate him, he would pay for me to telephone him or even visit him in Sweden.

I left the restaurant in deep thought and started to drive home, trying to remember to which city in Sweden my philosophy professor had moved. Suddenly, I slammed on the brakes. I had carelessly entered a pedestrian crosswalk. A man was in the crosswalk and had been nudged slightly by my car. With my whole body shaking uncontrollably, I got out to see if he was hurt.

The pedestrian I had nearly knocked over was my philosophy professor from San Jose State University! He was on a layover between airline flights, on his way back to Sweden, and had decided to come into the UCLA area to buy some shoelaces.

With tears streaming down my face, I asked him whether or not I should become a doctor. He instantly recognized me. He did not even mention that I could have killed him, and that my car was now blocking traffic, with other drivers honking incessantly. When he said in a stern voice, "Yes, Andrea, you should become a doctor," I finally found the courage to commit.

Today, I love being a physician. I specialize in emergency medicine and pre-hospital emergency care, which my friends view as one of the more "ugly" and less feminine branches of medicine. I no longer have my childhood fears. To me, this is a most beautiful profession.

Healing does take place in modern medicine. Healing takes place everywhere. It happens any time that people care about one another. Aesthetics abound in medicine. It only takes seeing people for their souls, rather than their body parts.

As I drink my Sleepy Time tea and reflect on the day, I again thank those who stood in my way when I was trying to turn my back on this most honorable profession.

Andrea Eberly, M.D., is a board-certified emergency medicine physician who served for several years as the EMS Medical Director of the Island of Guam, during which time she wrote this story. She now lives in New Jersey with her husband and daughter and works as an editor-in-chief for the emergency medicine section of a medical software company. In her free time, she enjoys teaching, writing, and playing with her family.

In the Still of the Night

By Maria Lado

As I turned the corner the wind caught my coat, flinging it open. Quickly, I pulled it closed, shivering that winter evening in Melbourne in 1992. People hurried past, intent on their destinations. I wondered if they all had somewhere to sleep.

Heading for the back of the Krush Café, where I knew I could get a decent meal, I knocked on the peeling, blue-painted door. Old Maka opened it, smiling when he saw me.

"Hello there, little lady," he said. "Come on in out of the cold and I'll get you something. Hungry?"

"I sure am." I sat on the chair near the back door, looking around. The kitchen was buzzing with activity. Meals were being pushed swiftly through a square opening in the wall into the dining area of the café. I loved the warmth of the kitchen, but especially savored the aroma of food being cooked.

Maka collected the plates coming back from the dining area, scraping the leftovers onto a fresh plate. He picked up a knife and fork and headed for me.

"Here you are," he beamed. "Dig into that. It's awful the way people waste food these days. This was hardly touched."

"Suits me," I murmured between mouthfuls. "Anyway, you get paid whether they eat it or not."

"Yep, you're right there," he agreed. "If you want any more, just give me a yell."

Old Maka was proprietor of the Krush Café, and he did a brisk trade this time of night. He prided himself on his "home-cooked" meals and the comfortable atmosphere of his café.

I had met him several weeks before when I left the hostel after running out of money and was bone-weary from fruitless job hunting. Wandering around, my belongings in a small case and my saxophone under one arm, I found myself in the café, asking for a job.

Maka was sympathetic enough, but his was a family business, and he just didn't need any help.

"You're welcome to a meal, though," he had said. "Come through to the kitchen."

He introduced me to his wife, Jada, and daughters, Maxee and Tamarah, then gave me a plate heaped with delicious stew.

"No charge," he insisted. "I can see you need it, and I'd like very much to think that someone would feed my girls if they were hungry."

"Let me help with the washing up, then," I offered, rising to my feet.

"Nonsense," Jada said briskly. "Sit down and eat."

After that, at Maka's suggestion, I would go by at around seven every night if I was in the neighborhood. Tonight I had come in a little later than usual, and the dinner rush was over. Maka and Jada had time to sit with me for a cup of coffee.

"Do you play, Keisha?" asked Maka, motioning to my saxophone in its worn-out case.

"A bit," I said. "I really love music."

We talked for a while, and I showed them my grandmother's brooch; she had given it to me when she was dying of cancer, and it had been extremely precious to her. She knew I would always treasure it.

"Are they diamonds?" Jada asked, touching it gently.

"Yes, and garnets. It's very old. My grandfather gave it to her on their first wedding anniversary."

"It's beautiful. Don't ever part with it, dear."

"Oh, I never will! I promised Gran I'd give it to my eldest daughter when she gets married, and I will."

"By the way, Keisha, I meant to tell you," Maka spoke up, "there's a job available at the fish and chips shop across the road."

"Oh, Pops! You know Treach is a real pig to work for," Tamarah cut in. "Girls never stay."

"Never mind," I said hopefully. "It's a job. Maybe I'll be the one to suit him. Thanks, Maka. I'll go over straight away."

Unfortunately, Tamarah was right about Treach. Girls were definitely his problem—the younger, the better. I lasted almost a week, which must have been a record. I became quite an expert at dodging him, but the day came when he caught me in a corner, and there was no escape—except out the door—permanently.

As I climbed the stairs to the travelers' lounge at Brownstone Station, I hoped I would be early enough to find a sofa for the night. Glancing at the clock, I saw it was only 3 p.m., so I might be lucky. But the regulars always arrived early, and some even evicted anyone sitting in "their spot."

I couldn't blame them; a sofa in the subway station was cheerless enough, but a whole lot better than a shop doorway.

I discovered a couch in the "Outkast" room, an area taken over by the homeless when the travelers' lounge was full, and counted myself lucky as the area was smaller and therefore warmer. I could also warm my hands under the hot water tap and the electric heater.

Just as I was drifting off to sleep, a heavy hand shook my shoulder.

"What do you think you're doin' here?" a rough voice demanded. "This is mine. Git!"

Stammering an apology, I stumbled out, heading for the first outside seat I saw.

As I sank down, a male voice came out of nowhere. "Wanna share my coat?" Startled, I looked around; he was about my age, and his smile looked as warm as the coat he was holding out toward me.

"Thanks." We huddled together under the heavy old army coat.

"Don't ever tangle with Kidada," he grinned. "She's one tough cookie."

"The Outkast Room?"

"Yeah. I saw her go in not long after you, so I waited to pick up the pieces. By the way, Keenen's the name."

"I'm Keisha, and ... thanks."

We talked for a while, and he told me he had come down from the country, but could not find a job, no matter how hard he tried. Now his money had run out.

"My folks can't have me back," he said. "Since Pops lost his job, it's been hard on the family. The dough doesn't go very far."

"I know what you mean," I replied. "My pops was laid off, too, so I thought I could help by getting a job, but it's hopeless."

His eyes fell on my saxophone. "Do you play?"

"Well, a bit, and I sing in the mall some afternoons. It brings in a few dollars, if I'm lucky."

Gradually, the warmth from our bodies and the coat lulled us to sleep, and despite the hard wooden bench under me, my sleep was sweet and dreamless.

I awoke with a start the next morning to find myself alone. As I sat up, rubbing my freezing legs, I glanced down. "My sax!" I gasped. It was gone. Frantically, I searched my pockets for my brooch—it was also gone!

"Oh, Keenen, how could you?" But I knew the answer. He was just as desperate as the thousands of other homeless kids in the city. I sat there, shattered. What could I do?

I calmed down and started to think. The saxophone was gone, but maybe, just maybe, I could find the brooch. Keenen would either have sold or pawned it. Perhaps if I inquired at every pawn shop in the city, I might find it—but I still couldn't redeem it.

"Find it first," I told myself.

Luckily, most of the city pawn shops were in the same area: Russell Street. So I began my long walk. There was no hurry; once Keenen had the money for the brooch, it wasn't going anywhere –unless someone bought it! A fresh wave of panic hit me. The thought of anyone else owning my brooch was unthinkable.

Quickening my steps, I finally reached Russell Street, and began to work my way through the shops. Several hours later, I had lost all hope. With just one more pawn shop to visit, my feet hurt and my legs ached like never before. Entering the dingy little shop, I asked my question again.

"Do you have a diamond and garnet brooch that was brought in today?"

The proprietor shook his head.

Sadly, I left Russell Street, intending to return to the subway station. Maybe I could find Keenen. Surely he would tell me the whereabouts of my brooch when I explained how important it was to me.

As I wandered along Black Street, I saw a small arcade that I hadn't noticed earlier. Out of curiosity, I strolled in. There, in a tiny second-hand jewelry shop window, my brooch glimmered among various other pieces.

I couldn't believe it! As I stood, my head whirling with relief, an old man came out to gather his outside display, and I realized it was closing time. I stepped forward.

"Excuse me," I said. He looked up, his eyes questioning. "That brooch in the window ... may I see it?"

"Of course." He led the way into the shop and lifted the brooch from the window shelf, holding it toward me. I leaned forward.

"May I hold it? It's all right, really. I just want to hold it."

There must have been something in my voice that he trusted. It certainly wasn't my appearance.

"Well, all right." He handed it to me, and I turned it over. The name "Amelia," my grandmother's name, was inscribed on the back.

The old man quoted the price, and my heart sank. "It's very valuable, you know," he explained. "I expect it will sell quickly. Perhaps you would like to call the next time you're in town?"

For the next few days, I couldn't keep away from the little jewelry shop. I spent my days gazing in the window, afraid someone would buy my brooch.

Eventually, the old man invited me in, and we talked as I held my brooch, just a little at first. Then, as the days went by, we became friends. His name was Teddee Whittaker, and he ran the little shop alone since his wife had been hospitalized nearly a year ago.

"That brooch was yours, wasn't it?" he asked one morning.

"How did you know?"

"Oh, I can tell."

So I told him about the brooch, about my grandmother, about Keenen and my saxophone; even about my family, and my struggle to find a job. At the end, there was silence.

"I'm feeling puckish," he said at last. "Would you go across to the tea shop for me? Get something for yourself, too. I hate to eat alone."

As we ate and drank, he said, "Keisha, you could have grabbed that brooch and run any time in the last few days. I couldn't have stopped you."

"I wouldn't do that, Mr. Whittaker," I said quickly. "Although I must say it did occur to me once in the beginning. But you bought it in good faith, and it's yours now."

He filled his pipe carefully. "Yesterday I heard that my wife has died." I opened my mouth, but he held up his hand.

He continued, "No, don't say anything. She was a good woman, but she was sick a long time." He paused. "Now this is my idea. I have to go away for a few days—make some arrangements, you understand. Would you do me a favor and look after the shop while I'm gone?"

"Would I?" I was elated.

"You'll be paid, of course. Then, when I return, I may have a proposition for you. The shop is getting a bit too much for me these days. I'm getting too old now."

"Do you mean you're giving me a job? A real job?" I could hardly bear to ask.

"Would you like that? It would certainly help me out, and you would be ideal for the position. You could buy your brooch back, too, if you wish. At the price I paid for it, naturally."

"Oh, Mr. Whittaker! I kissed his dear old cheek. Life was good after all.

THE MYSTERY OF FATE:

Maria Lado works daily in financial planning as a practice manager in Sydney, Australia. She has been writing for as long as she can remember, and has written and staged a number of productions. She recently set up Sierra Productions to pursue various opportunities. However diverse her work and writing lives are, Maria finds one as satisfying as the other. She also finds time to share her blessings with others through her involvement in her local church, community, and various charities. This story is about one of Maria's best friends, Keisha. The title is taken from one of Keisha's favorite songs, "In the Still of the Night," which she used to play on her saxophone.

The Rosary

By Ann Wilkes

As surely as the law of gravity ensures that the apple will fall to the ground, God puts people in our paths at precisely the right moment for our mutual benefit.

"She's your sister," Dad said of the girl in the old photographs. "Her name is Sharon Pamela. She was your age in this picture."

I peered at the black and white graduation photo on the next page of the photo album. How amazing it felt to have a grown-up sister.

"Where is she?" I asked curiously.

"I don't know. I've lost touch with her over the years," Dad replied.

At eight years of age, that satisfied me. After I grew up, however, I was full of questions, although it was too late to ask, since my dad had died when I was sixteen.

My mother told me, "When you were a baby, Sharon's mother called your dad to tell him he was a grandfather, but all he could talk about was you."

When I was in my twenties, I had occasionally toyed with the idea of finding Sharon, but this was before the days of the Internet, and since I didn't know her married name, it meant I would have had to hire a detective. And maybe she didn't want to be found. She might resent me because Dad boasted about me that time her mother called, instead of showing an interest in Sharon's newborn baby. I always thought it would be great to have a sister, but she was twenty years older than I!

When I was going through my mother's things after she died in 1989, a decade after my dad died, I found a beautiful rosary. It could have been something Mom picked up on one of her many thrift store shopping trips, or something handed down through the family. Dad was raised Catholic, but it surely wasn't his. He didn't even believe in the Bible. I knew because I had asked him once while sitting on his lap helping him work crossword puzzles when I was ten.

"It's just a bunch of fairy tales," he had said.

Dad's parents came to America from the Azores around 1900. My father hadn't embraced his Portuguese heritage, and the only Portuguese I had ever heard him speak was the phrase *"mais para mim,"* meaning "more for me." I was a picky eater, so he said it to me often at the dinner table.

The rosary could have belonged to his mother or his sister, Mabel, but my grandparents and all nine of their children were dead. And when I asked my cousins, they didn't know anything about the rosary.

Bereft of both parents and most of my aunts and uncles, I felt like an orphan. By the year 2000 I had Internet access, which I used to search for long-lost cousins who still embraced their Portuguese roots, to fill that familial void. My Internet searches failed to turn up any lost cousins; just some names and a few dates for my great-grandparents and their parents. In the course of my genealogical research, however, I learned to look for the person I had information about in order to find others. Thus, I decided to try to locate my sister by first finding her mother.

I had put off going through my mom's papers after she died. She did not throw anything away, and the whole prospect was daunting. But I thought there might be something that would help when I was tracing my genealogy on the Internet. When I finally started going through her papers, I found many photographs and documents belonging to my dad, including a letter from his ex-wife's attorney saying my dad was absolved of financial responsibility for Sharon, due to her adoption by her stepfather. That one yellowing page had his ex-wife's maiden name, her married name, and her attorney's address. This information still wouldn't have helped much if Sharon's mother had moved out of state or had a common name—or had died. Thank God her name was Dola May.

I did a quick "people search" on the Internet for California and found a listing for one Dola May Storey, which gave an address. Armed with this information, I searched the Internet white pages for a telephone number. My sister still might not want to know me, but I had only spent five minutes on the search, and no money. At least I would never regret not having tried to find her.

I pushed the buttons on the telephone with shaking fingers. I got an answering machine with an old man's voice. I left a detailed message, then waited on pins and needles for a response.

A call came the following morning from a woman whom I later learned was Sharon's adopted sister, Donna. She didn't sound too eager to give me Sharon's phone number, but she finally did. I dialed the number.

An answering machine again! How does one leave such a message? This is what I said: "Hi. My name is Ann Wilkes, but I grew up as Kathryn Ann Bettencourt. You may or may not want to know me, but if you are the daughter of Dola May Storey and Lewis L. Bettencourt, we're half-sisters. Please call me."

I left my number. My husband, Pat, and I went to church, then out to Papa's Taverna for dinner with friends. Pat returned home early while I stayed for Greek folk dancing with our friends. I didn't want to go home and sit, waiting for the phone to ring.

When I finally got home, my husband and son bombarded me with, "Your sister called! Your sister called!"

Pure joy filled my soul. No one had ever spoken those words to me before. She had, in fact, called twice, and talked to my husband for some time. She was delighted! I called her back, and we talked for at least an hour.

Sharon's mother, Dola, had told her that our dad died a long time before he actually did, and she had never told her about me. She apparently did not want Sharon to look for him. Sherry, as she was known, thought he didn't love her. Well, if all those photographs he kept of her were any indication, it just wasn't true. Times were different then. There were no joint custody arrangements, and he'd been replaced by her stepfather.

Sherry had been on an odyssey of her own, reconnecting with the faith of our paternal grandmother, whom she called Nana; a grandmother I had never known because she'd died before I was born. Sherry had been forbidden by her mother to pursue Nana's faith, Catholicism, when she was growing up. Now, after spending a year as a catechist, Sherry was to be baptized in the Roman Catholic Church at the end of that month, April 2001, the day before Easter. What better time to meet in person! She lived in southern California, a short flight from our home in the Bay Area. I brought a scrapbook of our dad and his family, containing duplicates of documents and certificates, pictures of him and pictures of her with his handwriting on the back.

And the rosary.

I still didn't know whose it was, or even if it *was* a family heirloom, but I thought it a fitting baptism gift.

I parked the rental car and walked toward Sherry's apartment. There she was on the landing outside her front door, her white hair falling across her shoulders and halfway down her back. She looked like our Aunt Eva. And she was my sister! Neither of us knew what to do next. We were strangers, yet sisters. She invited me in.

She looked at the scrapbook, and I handed her the rosary.

"This was Nana's!" she exclaimed, her eyes sparkling. "I remember her wearing it when I was on her lap. Oh, thank you, Ann, thank you. And thank God for bringing us together. You have no idea how much this means to me."

And so the torch of our grandmother's faith, in the form of that rosary, passed on to my sister, who would never have known to look for me because she had not known of my existence. When Sharon was baptized the following day, she had Nana's rosary and a picture of Dad in her pocket. And I, her sister, looked on with love.

Thank you, God, for my sister. And thank you, Nana, wherever you are, for praying for your granddaughters.

Ann Wilkes lives in Sonoma County, California's wine country, with her husband and their youngest son, where she pursues her long-time dream of writing sci-fi. Ann's first novel, *Awesome Lavratt* (2008) is a tongue-in-cheek space opera involving mind control, passion and adventure. Her stories have appeared in online magazines and print anthologies.

While a departure from Ann's usual writing, "The Rosary" came from her heart. Visit her on the web at www.annwilkes.com. She also maintains a blog at sciencefictionmusings.blogspot.com.

Time for Life

By Jill Ronsley

Fate is a train roaring down the track of life. Sometimes you step off the track, and unless you look back over your shoulder and see the train go roaring past, you don't know what you missed.

Brenda Warneka

The Great Western Express was running its usual route to central London through Reading, Southall, Hanwell, and Ealing, terminating at Paddington Station. Commuters from the West Country relied on the fast train to reach the hub of England's metropolis.

It was 7:25 on a cool autumn morning. Alison prepared to leave for work. She and her children, Thomas and Madeleine, lived in a modest attached house with a small garden, delightfully called a "terraced house" in England. Only two weeks earlier, Alison had begun a new job as secretary for the legal director of a real estate agency in Nottinghill Gate, a prestigious, trendy part of London. This was the first job that she had had that gave her financial peace of mind. For the last ten years, she had struggled as a single parent to make ends meet by doing part-time hospital and secretarial work in her hometown of Ealing. Now she was working in posh central London, making almost three times as much money, and she could hardly believe her good luck!

Delayed while preparing the children for school, Alison hurried to catch the train at the West Ealing railway station, just a ten-minute walk from home.

Alison's nephew, Adam, her brother John's son, frequently took the same train to work from Reading, about fifty miles west of London. A cool dude and an accomplished musician, Adam had graduated from Brighton College that summer and quickly obtained a lucrative position as program developer, part of a think-tank for a new television channel called Basil TV Productions. Well on his way to a successful career, he was full of enthusiasm for his new prospects.

Alison dashed up Manor Road past the shops, over the bridge that crossed the railway lines, and along the other side. Approaching the station house, she looked beyond it toward the railway platform. Suddenly, the expression on her face turned to dismay. There was her train pulling away from West Ealing, picking up speed. She watched in disbelief as it zoomed off into the distance toward Paddington.

"Damn! I'll be late for work," she muttered. A few other frustrated commuters had missed the train, too. They would all have to wait for the next one.

They waited, but the next train did not come. A short while later, there was an announcement on the platform loudspeaker. There would be no more trains into the city that morning. Commuters would have to go to Ealing Broadway and catch the tube on the underground Central Line. They could take the bus to the subway station, but it was rush hour, and a brisk twenty-minute walk would get them there more quickly.

Now it was clear that Alison would be very late for work, and she began to worry. How could she have been so stupidly, haplessly late for the train when she had just started such a fine job and was desperately trying to make a good impression on her boss? Before catching the tube at Ealing Broadway, she had to find a telephone to let the office know she was on her way.

An hour earlier in Reading, Adam left home to catch the Great Western Express. As he approached the station, he glanced at his watch, and a glint of copper caught his eye. There on the sidewalk lay a penny, shining up at him, beckoning. "A lucky penny!" he fancied as he reached down to pick it up. Happily, he dropped it into his pocket and continued toward the station.

When Adam arrived, the train was already there. He strode across the platform to one of the carriages and grabbed the handle to open the door. As his fingers closed around the metal grip, the train's automatic locking system engaged. The doors of every car were locked instantly. *This can't be happening!* he thought, but there was nothing at all that he could do. He worked the handle two or three times in vain, and then turned on his heels, furious with himself. Had he arrived a moment earlier, he would have been on his way to London.

The time he had taken to pick up that "lucky" penny had caused him to miss his train. He reached into his pocket and flung the penny across the platform with contempt. Now he would have to wait for the next train, and he would be late for work.

At 8:30 a.m., Adam's father, John, a retired hydraulics engineer, turned on the television at home in Reading to watch the morning news. Suddenly, his face turned ashen.

The BBC reported breaking news of what would soon be known as the most disastrous train crash in the United Kingdom in forty-two years. On October 5, 1999, as the Great Western Express approached Paddington on one of the busiest sections of Britain's railway network, the westbound Thames train was leaving the terminal. It turned off a minor outbound line to continue onto a faster track, maneuvering across the inbound line traveled by the Great Western. The red stoplight was lit, but the Thames train did not heed the signal. The Great Western Express crashed head-on into the Thames train, causing explosions, fire, chaos, and destruction. Many passengers were trapped behind the electronically locked doors of the train. At least seventy people were killed and a hundred and fifty injured.

"Adam! Oh dear God!" Uncontrolled fear seared through John's veins. "And Alison! What about Alison?" He was trembling, nearly crazed with panic. "This can't be! No, this can't be happening to my family!"

And it wasn't. What had caused Alison to be just a few minutes late for the train when she was so eager to reach her new job on time? What made Adam stop for an insignificant piece of copper discarded on the sidewalk? Fate had worked its magic on this favored family, saying "Live on!"

When Alison heard about the train crash, she felt protected and blessed. Adam realized that he had indeed picked up a very lucky penny. Later that month, when the family celebrated John's sixty-first birthday, they all looked into each other's eyes and knew that good fortune was surely theirs.

Jill Ronsley, founder of Sun Editing & Book Design, is an award-winning editor who has worked on a plethora of books for children and adults, both fiction and nonfiction. She works for small- and medium-size publishers as an editor, book designer, and typesetter. Children's picture books that she has edited and designed were finalists in the Benjamin Franklin Awards 2008 for interior design and the New York Book Festival 2007. Visit her website www.suneditwrite.com for more information.

A Book from the Sealed Library

By Xujun Eberlein

Had I not "borrowed" a book from a sealed library during China's Cultural Revolution, and had a master lathe worker not come to oversee my middle school class, I never would have gotten my Ph.D. from MIT.

It was 1970 when I entered Chongqing's 29th middle school. Schools had been closed in China since the beginning of the Cultural Revolution in 1966, an era in which books were burned or seized instead of being read. Now schools were being reopened under a new authority: the Workers' Propaganda Team. Red banners hung everywhere in the schoolyard proclaiming "The Working Class Rules Everything!"

Master Yoe, a taciturn lathe worker in his late forties, was the WPT member stationed in my classroom. Without notice, he would randomly walk into our chatty classroom with his hands clasped behind him, sauntering around between our desks. Wherever he stopped, the noise in that area also stopped. Whenever I asked a teacher about anything, be it class schedules or other activities, the answer was invariably, "Ask Master Yoe."

I had never seen Master Yoe read anything, not even a newspaper. I suspected that he was illiterate. Until he caught me reading one day, that is.

I had had no books to read for several years. As soon as the Cultural Revolution began, my mother, the superintendent of a school district, sold all her books (except the works of Marx, Engels, Lenin, Stalin, and Chairman Mao) as waste paper to a salvage station. If we did not get rid of the books, she told me the Red Guards would come to raid our house. The books were considered "The Four Olds"—*old thought, old culture, old tradition, old custom*—and had to be swept out.

One day during my first year in middle school, I noticed a crack on the seal across the door of the one-room library. The library was located on the second floor of the office building at which my father, before his "disgrace," had been a department head of a government institute. Because of his former position, he was now labeled a "capitalist roader." I had to pass the office building, which was in the same complex as the apartment building in which we lived, on the way in or out of our yard, so I often wandered around inside it.

Like other libraries in China at the time, the door of this library was sealed by two long, narrow strips of white paper, pasted in an X, bearing black dates and red stamps on them, the official seal of closing by the Red Guards. For some reason, there were still shelves full of books inside. That much I could see through the chink in the door. Every once in a while, I would peek inside when no one was watching and fantasize about owning all those books.

When I noticed a tear appearing on the sealing strip, I told myself it wasn't because my forehead had pushed against it so many times. The tear grew wider each day. I "accidentally" passed by the door more frequently and stole glances at the tear's slow evolution. At last, one day, I saw that the sealing strip was about to snap. With a little extra push, surely it would.

I don't remember providing the push. It must have been a natural force that finally tore the seal. In any case, I found myself inside the dim, dusty library, standing in front of spider-webbed bookshelves. Not daring to stay long, I grabbed a thick, tattered book from the nearest shelf. *It must be an interesting book if so many people have read it,* I thought. Hiding the book under my shirt, I snuck out, heart pounding, and ran home.

The book was *Three Kingdoms.* While virtually all books belonged to The Four Olds, this was the epitome of them—one of the oldest classic novels. Before the Cultural Revolution began, I had heard fragments of the novel when in teahouses with my parents, told by folk storytellers holding a short piece of wood board to strike the table and make a loud noise whenever the story was approaching a climax. For several afternoons after school, I immersed myself in the novel. No one interrupted me. I was in heaven. Only my illiterate and affectionate grandmother, who had great respect for written words and would tiptoe around whenever I was reading, and my younger sister—a muddy-headed ten-year-old who was content to leave me alone as long as I promised to tell her a story I'd read—were at home.

I laughed when Zhuge Liang, the greatest war strategist, tricked his enemy with the "Empty City Ruse" and "borrowed" the enemy's arrows using straw boats; I cried when he died of sickness on an autumn night with his army's victory within arm's reach. I saw nothing but the ancient regiment flags and shining spears; I heard nothing but the beat of battalion drums and the neighs of armored horses. I wished I had been born in that heroic time. My dream was broken only by my parents returning home from their work units each day, at which point I quickly stashed the book under my quilt. My parents, laden with their own burdens, noticed nothing.

Against my better judgment, I brought the book to school a few days later, spellbound by the final chapters. I knew very well that the book had the stamp of my father's work unit on it.

Although being castigated, he was still a member of the same work unit as before the Cultural Revolution, and was required to report to the office every day to participate in denouncement sessions held by those who had formerly worked under him. If caught by the WPT with the book, I would not only bring disaster on myself, but also impose a new crime upon my father's name for allowing me to have a forbidden book.

I was dying to know if Zhuge Liang's chosen successor, Jaing Wei, had won the war. Sitting down at my desk, I carefully opened the book in the compartment under my desktop; I kept my head up, lowering my eyes only to read. Every few minutes, I glanced around to see if anyone was watching. The classroom was like the ruckus in a hornet's nest—all my classmates were chatting, kidding, throwing chalk around, and no one paid attention to the poor teacher writing whatever on the blackboard, let alone to me. More reassuring still, Master Yoe wasn't in the classroom.

I could stay alert to my surroundings for only so long when reading such an enticing book. After a dozen pages, I became so engrossed in the story that I forgot everything else, until the blue veins on a big hand filled my eyes and took the book, almost gently, away. I looked up, panic stricken, meeting Master Yoe's serious gaze. God knows when he had walked in.

One day, months later, a group of men arrived at our school in green military dress. With their arrival, new slogans appeared on the campus walls: "Station troops to guard the frontier and cultivate the borderland!" The "troops," it turned out, meant us middle school students. We were being recruited to go to Yunnan, on China's southern border next to Burma, to plant rubber trees on army reclamation farms. Anyone who had turned sixteen was eligible, which meant most of the students, since they had been delayed by several years without schools. The recruiters would be pleased if we all joined them.

My best friend and I hit palms, pledging to go together. We applied enthusiastically, as did many of our friends. Every regime has its own politically correct terms. What we did was politically correct, expected, and honorable in our time.

When I handed my application—one page full of vehement words—to Master Yoe, he said, "You are not sixteen yet."

"In three months, I will be. Revolution does not discriminate by age!" I replied fiercely.

"We'll need your parents' agreement," he told me. His swarthy face showed no smile.

I was confident that my mother, a Party member, would support my correct decision. But she turned out to be tough. She said I was too young. Yunnan was too far away, work on an army reclamation farm would be too hard, and much more. I pestered her day after day, alternating cajolement with coercion and crying. Finally, she sighed.

"All right, go. It will happen sooner or later." She knew she would not be able to keep me in the city after my graduation anyway. My elder sister had already been sent to the countryside for "re-education." I could see how sad my mother was that I did not want to wait even one more year, but a mother's sadness was not a teenager's concern.

I rushed back to school to find Master Yoe. I told him my good news, speaking incoherently as I panted for breath. He looked suspicious. "Really? Your mother agreed?" I just couldn't understand his lack of excitement, but at least he did not turn me down.

In a few weeks, the school announced a list of students approved to go to Yunnan in a broadcast over a loudspeaker and a posting on a big wall, where the names studded the paper like ants. Everyone I knew who applied got their wish, including my best friend, but I did not find my name. Did this mean I was not trustworthy?

Master Yoe wore a sly smile when I confronted him. "Shh. You are not going to Yunnan. You are going to high school."

That was the first time I heard the news that high schools would reopen. High schools had not been needed because universities admitted only factory workers, peasants, and soldiers by recommendation, many of them semi-literates. Now, Master Yoe told me secretively that Chinese Premier Zhou Enlai had instructed that there was to be an "experiment" (as if it were a novelty): to admit a small number of students to high school. As such, my school was in the process of selecting *one* student from each class to go to high school. And Master Yoe had singled me out from my thirty-plus classmates.

That fateful day when Master Yoe seized my *Three Kingdoms*, I did all I could to plead with him to give it back to me. I vowed to become the most obedient, disciplined, and well-behaved student, and do whatever he asked me to do. I begged him not to implicate my father.

"I'll tell you my decision in three days," he had said.

It was an odd thing to say. What would take him three days to decide? But a delayed decision was certainly better than an immediate execution. I nodded meekly, as if in a position to disagree.

There is no need to describe how heavily time hung on me during those three days; it taught me the meaning of an old adage: "Live a day as if it were a year." The third afternoon, I followed Master Yoe to a quiet corner on campus and timidly reminded him of the deadline.

He handed me the book rolled in a newspaper and said, "Nice, nice. I've been looking for this book for some time. Never thought it would arrive so easily." He smacked his lips like a glutton. "Here you are, girl. Don't let me see it again."

He had taken the novel for three days to read himself.

Afterward, Master Yoe and I discussed Zhuge Liang, the embodiment of Chinese wisdom. I believe this was why he wanted to see me go on to high school: for our shared secret love of *Three Kingdoms*.

That was how my infatuation with books frustrated my political correctness. With the help of a worker whose duty was to demolish old books, I went to high school instead of a rubber tree farm. Luckily, my high school years overlapped with Deng Xiaoping's short-lived "second time up" as China's vice-premier, and under new policies issued by our country's practical leaders Zhou and Deng, I had an almost normal education in the sciences and literature.

After the Cultural Revolution ended and universities finally reopened to the public, in the winter of 1977, I took China's most heavily-attended national college entrance exam in history, administered to a decade's accumulation of wannabe students, many of whom had never set foot in high school. I passed the exam with high scores and was accepted at Chongqing University. Far away in Yunnan, my best friend from middle school, a bright girl who had joined a rubber tree farm seven years earlier, also took the exam; but she did not pass. She later returned to Chongquing when, after repeated entreaties, demonstrations, and hunger strikes, the millions of city youths brought to Yunnan from Beijing, Shanghai, Chengdu, and Chongqing were finally allowed to go home. She never spoke to me again after she learned of my college admission.

As it turned out, none of my middle school classmates got into university. Only then did I realize what a great favor Master Yoe, whose full name I never learned, had done for me.

Xujun Eberlein grew up in Chongqing, China, moved to the United States in 1988, and received her Ph.D. from MIT in 1995. She has won many awards for her fiction and literary non-fiction works, which

have been published in the United States, Canada, England, Kenya, and Hong Kong. Her debut story collection, *Apologies Forthcoming*, which won the 2007 Tartt Fiction Award, was published in 2008. Xujun can be reached through her website www.xujuneberlein.com.

Miracle in Alexandria

By Vicka Markov Surovtsov

Yet who shall shut out fate?
Edwin Arnold

Life is a series of big and small miracles. We tend to take them for granted, but there are some that stay in our minds forever.

My family, Russian in origin, immigrated to Alexandria, Egypt, from its homeland in 1920. I was born the following year. We were stateless since we were never required to become Egyptian citizens, and were under the protection of the Royal House of Egypt. However, when Farouk, the last king of Egypt, was overthrown and exiled in 1956, we were uneasy as to our future, even though we did not belong to the group of Farouk supporters who were being deported.

It was April 1958: Alexandria was in turmoil. Following the war with Israel, there was a general exodus of foreign nationals, such as English, French and anybody of the Jewish faith. The political climate in the country was strongly fomented by Muslim extremists who were putting pressure on the authorities to get rid of all foreigners on Egyptian soil.

My father was a captain with the Anglo-Egyptian police, and continued as such after the takeover of the country by the military headed by General Mohammed Neguib and later by Colonel Abdel Nasser. However, we decided to seek refuge in the United States. The Russian quota, being very small, allowed us to obtain American visas in record time. Father put in his resignation, but stress and worry took their toll, and he had a near-fatal heart attack. He recuperated slowly, but kept his spirits high, knowing he was about to take his family out of a country where we were no longer welcome.

One morning close to our departure date, my father and I took a taxi to the passport office to collect our papers. We would then proceed downtown to the shipping company that was sending our heavy trunks full of books and personal articles to the United States. We were also to collect our passage tickets on the ship that was taking us to New York because Father's health did not permit him to fly. We had a large amount of money with us since we could not write checks, as our British bank account was sequestrated (though we were able to withdraw our savings just in time), and all transactions had to be made in cash. I carried a large leather attaché case containing our precious American visas, the money, and my father's big police revolver, still in its halter, which was to be returned to his office the same day.

We asked the taxi driver to wait for us while we collected the passports, which we then placed in the case, and directed the driver to go to the shipping company on Sherif Pasha Street, in the center of the busy downtown area. Father was very nervous because we were carrying the revolver. During those dangerous days, it was a criminal offense to carry any firearm, and people were pitilessly jailed for less than that. However, we hoped that we would soon consign the revolver to the Central Precinct before anyone would spot it.

We arrived at our destination and went up the ancient elevator to the third floor of the massive old building, built at the turn of the century. Greeted by the friendly manager of the shipping company, Father sank into a comfortable chair and asked me to hand him the attaché case. For a long moment, I stared at my father's face while my mind tried to cope with the realization that we no longer had the case!

We looked at each other in horror, unable to speak. I had believed that Father was holding the case, while he had thought I was carrying it. While getting out of the taxi and paying the driver, neither of us noticed that the attaché case had been left in the taxi!

Father leaned back in his chair and closed his eyes. I knew the loss of the attaché case meant that we had lost everything. We had already sold our house, our furniture and our car. Our passports, our only identification now, were gone. Our money, our American visas, and, more ominously, the service revolver were gone.

There was little hope of the taxi driver ever returning the contents of the case. Even the most honest of men would be too frightened to admit that he had a revolver, which could land him directly in jail.

Unwilling to wait for the elevator, I rushed down the stairs and into the busy street. All taxi cabs were yellow, and there were dozens of them speeding in opposite directions while I looked around in despair. The sidewalks were crowded with shoppers and peddlers who jostled me. I prayed to God, unable to remember any proper words of prayer, but hoping He would understand my turmoil and helplessness.

I jumped as a hand grabbed my arm, and I looked into the laughing face of a friend of ours, whose office was in the business district. "Hey," he said, "what the heck are you doing here instead of packing your belongings?"

I could not control the tears that streamed down my face as I told him in a few jumbled sentences what had happened. He questioned me as to whether I remembered anything about the taxi or the driver, but all I could tell him was that we had picked him up on the street and asked him to wait for us at the passport office.

My friend hailed a passing taxi and told the driver to go to the passport office. This was our only clue, weak as it was. Arriving at the intersection of the government office, we saw a long line of yellow taxis, all identical, all drivers looking like clones of our former driver. We got out and started walking toward the waiting cabs.

All of a sudden, one of the drivers thrust his head through his window and shouted, "Mademoiselle, Mademoiselle, where do you want to go this time? I'll take you!"

I thought I would pass out from the anxiety. We rushed toward the taxi, and my friend quickly opened the back door. There, flat on the floor, half-concealed under the back of the driver's seat, lay our precious attaché case, still bulging with its priceless contents.

I will never forget the expression of disappointment on the face of the driver when he saw us pull out the attaché case and realized that he had failed to spot it. However, since he did not know what he had missed, we did not tell him. He accepted a generous tip and happily drove away, while I suddenly realized that God had indeed heard me, even though I had forgotten the proper words of prayer for this occasion.

I went back to the shipping company where I knew a moment of pure joy when I handed over the case to my dear father, who just held me in his arms for a while, wiping away my tears with his gentle hand.

Vicka Surovtsov, nee Markov, was born in Egypt. She has an M.A. in French and Russian, has traveled extensively in Europe and Latin America, and speaks five languages. She was married to the late George Surovtsov and she lives in Northern California. Her hobbies are portrait painting, chess, and writing. Her first book, a memoir, *Amigos & Friends*, is about her and George's very interesting life in Mexico, where they made many good friends. She is working at present on her second book, *Snow and Sand*, which embraces three generations of a family torn by passion and a merciless civil war.

Desert Boomerang

By Steven Manchester

In 1991, as a shield was replaced by an angry storm, Saddam Hussein threatened America with the mother of all battles. In turn, President George H. W. Bush drew a line in the sand. That line was quickly wrapped around Iraq and used to choke the life out of thousands. As a U.S. Army MP, I was there when the Americans crossed the breach from Saudi Arabia into Iraq, crushing the first of three Iraqi lines of defense along the way. It was like someone had lifted the curtain to hell, giving everyone a free peek.

It took four days, or a mere one hundred hours, before the ground war ended. History was made. In triumph, Kuwait was liberated while Hussein was humiliated before the whole world. An unconditional withdrawal was ordered. Politically, the sadistic demon was slain. In reality, unlike thousands of his own people, he still lived. And the war was far from over.

Two weeks after the last shots were fired, I was standing guard at a barren traffic control point in Iraq when a lone vehicle approached. It was American, so I waved it through. The driver pulled up to me and stopped. He was a black sergeant, and from the look in his eyes, he was definitely lost.

"Man, am I glad to see you!" he said with a nervous grin. "I lost my convoy in the dust storm that just passed through. I'm supposed to be on Main Supply Route Green, but…"

I chuckled. The entire area was my patrol and I could have driven the roads in Iraq blindfolded. "You're not that far off," I confirmed. "Right now, you're on MSR Blue, but this route runs parallel to MSR Green. Keep south for the next four miles or so, and when you reach a fork in the road, you've met up with Green."

The sergeant's face showed relief, and I was happy to help him. With a wave, he was on his way. I, on the other hand, returned to the boredom of the desert's miles and miles of solitary confinement.

Several very unpleasant months passed. One afternoon in base camp, my platoon sergeant, Tony Rosini, approached. "Hey, kid, got any plans today?"

"Yeah, I think I'll head to the mall," I joked.

He chuckled. "In that case, you can give me a ride into Saudi Arabia. My knee's been acting up, so maybe they'll give me some painkillers. Either way, I could use the time away, and from the look of it, so could you."

"Whose vehicle?" I asked.

Tony never answered. He just slid into the passenger seat of his own "A Horse With No Name."

We were making good time, traveling down the dusty road at a fast clip. We joked and laughed; there were only forty miles between the Saudi Arabian border and us. Before long, radio traffic ceased. We were out of range. I noticed we had been the only vehicle on the road since we left. I continually scanned the vast terrain to make sure we were alone. There were still members of Iraq's Republican Guard on the loose, soldiers who came out of hiding during the dark hours. The farther we drove, though, the less it mattered. We were only an hour from our destination and safety.

Several miles later, I slowed down. We'd hit a dust storm, a bad one. I could hardly see three feet past the windshield. In the blink of an eye, the blue sky turned a blinding orange as the harsh winds of the open desert rearranged the landscape.

Maneuvering the Humvee right and left, I slowed down even more on the serpentine trail. Squinting my eyes, I concentrated and drove on. Then the nightmare began.

Approximately thirty miles from the border, I heard the bang. I did not know the cause, but it was a loud crash that came from the right side of the vehicle. The cause didn't matter because the rest was out of my hands.

In super slow motion, the vehicle tipped left, toward the driver's side. The windshield cracked at the top, then spider webbed throughout the center. The desert spun in circles before my eyes. I felt something heavy smash into the back of my bare skull. It was an army field phone, flying around aimlessly until it found a target. The piercing pain quickly led to numbness. My tense body went limp.

I felt as if I was submerged in a pool of warm water. Unlike any peace I had ever experienced before, the sensation was heavenly. With no choice but to accept the comfort, my eyes slammed shut. In the briefest moment in time, I watched as my life played out before me. It was a slide show, with one vivid picture after another being brought into the light.

I was euphoric. I was at peace. Then, as if reality was given its last chance, I thought, *All of this, just to die in a Humvee accident?* I fought it off with everything inside me. I didn't want death. It wasn't my time. I fought, but the struggle was brief. There was no more pain, no more peace, no more pictures. There was only darkness.

I opened my eyes and felt a methodical pain surge throughout my being. My entire body throbbed, but it was my left arm and neck that caused me to groan. Attempting to lift my heavy head, my mind twirled in circles, fogged from the pain and disoriented from the shock. Turning my head slowly, I looked down at my fingers. My wedding band was missing. Turning right, I saw the Humvee. It was almost forty feet away, lying on its roof. It looked like a hapless turtle upside down, resting on its shell. With all my might, I pushed myself to my knees.

The Humvee's engine screamed for help. It was running at full idle. Trying to clear my blurred vision, I choked on the smell of gas and oil that leaked from the wreck. I had taken two small, painful steps toward the vehicle when I saw Tony.

Like a bat, my platoon sergeant hung upside down within the wreckage. He was suspended in mid-air by a seatbelt and appeared unconscious. He was in trouble. He needed help. Picking up the pace, I ignored my own pain.

"Get out! Tony, get out!" I shouted.

Tony never moved, but the engine seemed to hear me. It raced faster. Without hesitation, I dove into the Humvee.

I was right. Tony was out cold. I unbuckled the safety belt and awkwardly pulled my friend out. He was dead weight, but I continued to drag him, hoping that I wasn't causing more damage. I couldn't tell if Tony's back or neck was broken. Then, I realized that I wasn't even sure whether he was alive. I dragged him faster.

A safe distance from the vehicle, I laid him on the warm sand and took his pulse. He was still alive. Feeling the greatest sense of relief, I was promptly reacquainted with my own pain. The intensity made me nauseated. I felt as if I was going to pass out, but fought it off. Though I wanted nothing more, there was no time for a nap. Tony was coming out of it. The engine in the jeep let out one last whine and seized to an eerie halt.

For a while I just sat in the sand with Tony's head in my lap. He talked in riddles. His gibberish told me that he was in shock. I treated the symptoms according to my army training: I loosened Tony's restrictive clothing and elevated his feet. I moistened his lips with water. Bending over, I shaded my platoon sergeant's face from the burning sun.

Unsure whether he could understand or not, I also began reassuring my friend. It was the biggest act of my life, but I promised, "Don't you worry, Tony. I'll get us out of this one. We'll be okay." The empty words drifted off into the lonely desert. I was overcome with guilt; after all, I was behind the wheel when the accident occurred.

"My God, Tony, what have I done?" I whispered. Tony never answered. He just mumbled and shivered from the cold. The shiver scared me. It was more than ninety degrees and my friend was freezing. Removing my shirt, I covered his upper body, then headed back to the smashed Humvee.

I needed to figure out a plan. The closer I got to the vehicle, the easier it was to see that I was not responsible for what had happened. In the midst of the heavy dust storm, we had hit a boulder with the right front tire. The Humvee had flipped three or four times, completely crushing the driver's side. It finally landed on its roof. The driver's side door was lying twenty feet from the scene. My spine tingled when I saw it.

It was too bizarre to be coincidental. I hadn't been wearing a helmet, which had allowed the telephone to knock me out. Unconscious, my limp body had been thrown around at will. My seatbelt would have trapped me under the weight of the wreckage, but I had neglected to put it on. The door had flown off, throwing me out of the truck and away from the final landing. That was the clincher. If each element hadn't happened in sequence, I would have been smashed like a grape. For reasons unknown to me, I was still alive. It was no less than a miracle. From then on, I felt as if I was living on borrowed time. I didn't like the feeling.

Searching the ruined interior of the wreck, I was consumed with worry. We were in the middle of nowhere, with nothing but sand in all directions. There was no food and maybe enough water for six hours under the relentless sun. Worst of all, there was no means of communication! The antenna was buried under the wreck, and though I tried again and again to make contact over my radio with a medi-vac (emergency helicopter), it was no use. My pleas for help went unheard.

Nobody knew we existed. Even the boys at the base camp didn't expect us back for a whole day. There would be no search for at least that long. A helpless fear welled up inside me. I called for a medi-vac one last time. I waited. There was a terrible silence. We were alone! Fighting off despair, I grabbed my rifle, a box of ammo and a ragged blanket, and returned to Tony. The only thing left was faith, but I was losing even that. For me, there was no hope in sight.

Tony became more coherent and asked, "What the hell happened?"

I explained the accident, adding an apology at the end.

He raised his hands toward the sky. "You worry too much, Stevie Boy. Just get us the hell out of here!"

I smiled, and then lied, looking straight into my friend's frightened eyes. "No sweat, boss. I made the call. Help should be here in no time."

Tony said nothing. He just grinned weakly as he lapsed back into unconsciousness. Rocking him back and forth, I looked over at the wreck. The hopelessness tore at my very core. Looking down at my older friend, I knew it was better that Tony didn't know the truth; a truth which meant probable death.

There was nothing I could do. We were both in rough shape. Traveling on foot was impossible. The radio was no longer an option. The only thing to do was wait. I hated that lack of control. As the steady breezes covered Tony and me with sand, I felt as if we were sitting in an hourglass with our time running out. With all Allied forces heading farther north, the chance of someone driving past was extremely remote. Situated somewhere on the southern tip of Iraq, we were in big trouble.

The two longest hours of my life passed without a change in our dilemma. With each passing minute, the outcome looked more bleak. Tony drifted in and out of consciousness. I sat alone, wincing from physical pain and struggling with mental torment. It was too much. My platoon sergeant was getting worse, and there was nothing more I could do. The trauma tore me apart. I feared Tony's death more than my own. For the first time during the war, I cried.

I sobbed in despair, even self-pity. Time crawled by, though it was irrelevant. Tony was dying from his physical wounds, and I was all but dead inside myself. I'd never felt so broken. I had never wanted to die alone. Now I didn't have to.

An American vehicle appeared on the horizon. A miracle had been sent. The cavalry was on its way!

The hand of an angel rested upon my shoulder. Looking up, I stared into his face. A soldier bent down and gently whispered, "Lay down, Sarge. I'm gonna take care of you now. It's all over. We're gonna get you out of here." With that, he winked.

I couldn't believe it. It was the lost soldier I'd given directions to a few months before.

"But how did you ...?" I started.

He smiled. "Nice to see you again, too. After the directions you gave me, I finally found my medical unit." He looked back at the road. "I'm assigned to the scout vehicle. I'm about ten minutes ahead of our convoy. They should be along in a bit."

"So how did you know we were here?" I asked. "Did you hear my radio transmission?" I knew the Humvee's antenna was buried, yet there was no other logical explanation for his sudden appearance. At that time, in that place, it would have been a miracle for anyone to happen by.

"What transmission?" he replied. "We were just passing through."

In disbelief, I collapsed onto the hot sand. My throbbing body could finally rest; my tortured mind was at ease.

Sergeant Jason Matthews, a medic, called for a chopper, and then worked feverishly over me. I was strapped to a long-board while my pants and shoulder holster were completely cut off. My arm was splinted and my neck placed into a bulky brace. An IV was administered, and through it all, I slipped in and out of the real world.

Tony was also shoved into a cocoon of precautionary devices while an IV was stuck into his thirsty veins. After a few mumbled complaints, he fell asleep in the shadow of a praying army chaplain. I was relieved to find out that his condition was stable.

Before long, the medi-vac chopper flew in for the pick-up. After covering me from head to toe with a warm foil wrap, Sergeant Matthews placed his upper body over my face, shielding me from the blowing sand. Touching down, the airborne ambulance's motor was cut down to a high-pitched whine. It was the most welcome screech I had ever heard.

Four men lifted Tony up and rushed him toward the helicopter. Upon their return, the same men lifted up my canvas litter, and at a sprint, I was also rushed to the helicopter. Tony was fast asleep. Looking back at Matthews, I yelled, "Thank you!" though there was no way he could have heard me. The chopper was too loud.

With a look of urgency, though, Matthews ran over to me. He grabbed my hand and placed something into the palm. With a wonderful smile, he gave a thumbs-up and was gone. I opened my hand. It was my gold wedding band, slightly misshapen but shining brightly. Goosebumps erupted over my body. It was too unbelievable to be real, yet it was true. I had lived through it. I slid the ring back onto my finger and the chopper took to the air.

Miraculously, Tony and I both healed. I stayed in the Army until the Gulf War ended. Tony retired with a disability, and to this day he still offers to pay for driving lessons for me.

Steven Manchester is the published author of *Pressed Pennies, The Unexpected Storm, The Gulf War Legacy, Jacob Evan, A Father's Love, Warp II,* and *At the Stroke of Midnight,* as well as several books under the pseudonym Steven Herberts. His work is showcased in such literary journals as *Taproot Literary Review, American Poetry Review,* and *Fresh! Literary Magazine.* Steven is an accomplished speaker and currently teaches the popular workshop "Write a Book, Get Published, and Promote Your Work." Three of his screenplays have also been produced as films. He is the father of two sons and one beautiful little girl. When not spending time with his own children, writing, teaching, or promoting his published books and films, this Massachusetts author speaks publicly to troubled children through the Straight Ahead Program. www.StevenManchester.com.

The Amazing Tablecloth

As told by Rabbi Adam Glickman

Many families were separated by the Nazis during World War II, never to see each other again—at least not in this life. There were some survivors, however, who were fortunate enough to reconnect after the war, although in some cases, not until many years later.

How did these people find each other? Some through government agencies, others through networking or word of mouth, and still others, in more recent years, through the Internet.

But there were also those who found each other, perhaps after giving up the likelihood or possibility (but never the hope) of ever seeing one another again, through the "mystery of fate."

Following is one such story, told by Rabbi Adam Glickman, of the AG Beth Israel Synagogue in Chicago, Illinois, during a Rosh Hashanah (Jewish High Holy Day) service.

A rabbi and his wife relocated to a new synagogue. The couple arrived in early July, excited about their opportunities in this previously unknown community. The synagogue was rundown and needed a lot of work. Their goal was to be ready for Rosh Hashanah, one of the holiest of the Jewish holidays, which takes place in autumn. They worked very hard, repairing the Holy Ark, plastering the walls and painting the synagogue. They finished in mid-August, ahead of schedule.

Only a few days before Rosh Hashanah, a terrible driving rain hit the area, lasting two days. Immediately after the storm, the rabbi returned to his synagogue. His heart sank when he saw that the roof had leaked, causing a large area of plaster, about six-by-eight feet, to fall off the front wall of the sanctuary.

While cleaning up the mess, the rabbi asked God for a miracle. On his way home, he noticed a local business having a flea market sale for charity, so he stopped in. One of the items was a beautifully hand-crocheted tablecloth. It had fine colors and the Star of David embroidered in the center. It was just the right size to cover up the hole on the front wall.

Rushing back to the synagogue, he saw an older woman running to catch a bus she had just missed. The rabbi invited her inside to wait for the next bus. She sat in the sanctuary and paid little attention to him while he climbed a ladder to hang the tablecloth as a wall tapestry. It looked beautiful. Then he noticed the woman walking down the aisle. Her face was white as a sheet. "Rabbi," she asked, "where did you get that tablecloth?"

Before he had a chance to reply, she asked him to please check the lower right corner to see if the initials "EBG" were crocheted into it. They were.

These were the initials of the woman, and she had made this tablecloth some thirty-five years before, in Austria. The woman could hardly believe it as the rabbi told how he had just obtained the tablecloth. The woman explained that before the war, she and her husband were a well-to-do family. When the Nazis came, she was forced to leave. Her husband was going to follow the next week. She was captured, sent to a concentration camp, and never saw her husband or her home again.

The rabbi wanted to give her the tablecloth, but she told him to keep it for the synagogue. He insisted on driving her home, feeling that it was the least he could do. She lived on the other side of town and was only in the area for the day. Upon reaching her home, he graciously thanked her for the beautiful tablecloth, and she thanked him for the ride.

The following day, the Rosh Hashanah service was lovely. The synagogue was almost full, and the prayer sounds were like music. At the end of the service, everyone said to each other, "May you be written and inscribed in the Book of Life for a good year." One older man, whom the rabbi recognized from the neighborhood, continued to sit and stare at the wall. The rabbi wondered why he wasn't leaving. The man asked him where he had gotten the tablecloth on the wall because it was identical to the one his wife had made years ago when they lived in Austria. His wife's initials were "EBG."

The rabbi asked if the man would go for a ride with him. When he asked why, the rabbi just said to trust him; he would find out in good time. The man agreed and they drove to a house on the other side of town. The rabbi helped the man to the door and knocked. When the woman opened the door, the rabbi witnessed the most incredible reunion and biggest miracle he had ever seen.

The Quake That Made a Marriage

By Aimee Liu

Among the many improbable aftershocks of the Great San Francisco Earthquake and Fire of 1906 is one that led, if indirectly, to my existence. Just six weeks after the disaster, a wedding party of seven couples, which included four Chinese men and their American brides-to-be, set off from the Oakland train depot, prepared to violate California law. That small band of romantic rebels included my grandparents.

My grandfather Liu Ch'eng-yu was then thirty-one years old. He had come to San Francisco three years earlier by a circuitous route. The only son of the late viceroy of Canton under the Qing dynasty, Ch'eng-yu was classically trained as a poet and scholar, groomed to serve in government. But in his headstrong teens, he had resolved instead to overthrow China's imperial system. When his plot to blow up a local armory was exposed, he narrowly escaped being beheaded. He fled to Tokyo, where he fell under the sway of Dr. Sun Yat-sen, the revolutionary leader known today as the Father of Modern China.

Ch'eng-yu became so enamored with western-style freedom that he cut off his queue, the long hair braid that all Chinese men were required to wear as a show of submission to their Manchu rulers. He traded his scholar's robes for waistcoats and a bowler hat. On January 1, 1903, he stood up at a New Year's party in Tokyo and called for democracy in China, causing both the Japanese and Manchu officials who were present to lose face. Dr. Sun decided my grandfather should move to San Francisco, where he would edit the revolutionary newspaper *Ta T'ung Daily*.

There was just one problem: the Chinese Exclusion Act, which had been in effect since 1882 (and would not be repealed until 1943), forbade the Chinese to enter America. Exceptions were made for merchants with an established record of doing business in the United States and for students enrolled in American schools. All other Chinese were treated as laborers who "endangered the good order" of society, and so were denied entry. However, Dr. Sun knew how to pull certain strings through the Chinese Freemasons in Oakland, and he arranged for Ch'eng-yu to enter the country on a student visa and matriculate at UC Berkeley. My grandfather attended classes by day and beat the drum of China's revolution by night.

To keep up his studies, Ch'eng-yu needed tutoring in English. The university directed him to Jennie Ella Trescott, then twenty-five years old and single, living in a boarding house near the college. Jennie was a slender strawberry blonde, with luminous blue eyes and a misleadingly majestic air. Her erect posture and immaculate, high-necked white blouses belied her origins as an only child, born of pioneers in Fort Dodge, Kansas. Her mother had died of diphtheria when Jennie was two, leaving her to be raised by family friends. Jennie's father, though a generous, good-tempered man, failed first at cattle ranching and then at selling snake oil from a traveling medicine wagon. He loved his daughter, but could not support her. She might have found another man to support her through marriage, but Jennie was as headstrong as Ch'eng-yu. She chose college and independence. Just how she made this all happen is a gray area.

This did not mean, however, that Jennie was immune to the lure of men or of luxury. When her dapper and passionate Chinese pupil described the Forbidden City where he had taken his Imperial exams, and the caches of emeralds, rubies, and gold that his father had amassed during his service as viceroy, Jennie became enthralled. The contradiction between Ch'eng-yu's modern dress and politics and his exotic ancestry only made him more intriguing. The two of them joked that if she went with him to China, he would make her his "American princess."

Of course, there was no possibility of romance between them. In California, even scholarly Chinese belonged to a despised minority. Interracial courtship was taboo. Marriage between Chinese men and Caucasian women was against the law throughout the west. The last of America's anti-miscegenation laws would not be overturned until 1967. It took an earthquake to make my grandparents' union possible.

On April 18, 1906, across the Bay Area, all social conventions and laws were suspended when the Great San Francisco Earthquake hit. Streets cracked open. Houses split in two. Fire engulfed downtown San Francisco, forcing thousands to take refuge in Golden Gate Park or escape by the boatload to Sausalito or the East Bay. In the havoc, no one noticed or cared that a single white woman in Berkeley had accepted the protection of a Chinese man.

Chinatown in San Francisco, and with it the offices of *Ta T'ung Daily,* was reduced to ashes. No one knew when classes would resume at the university at Berkeley. The quake had left both Jennie and Ch'eng-yu homeless, but it had also left them, at least temporarily, liberated.

The nearest town where a Chinese man could marry a white woman in 1906 was Evanston, Wyoming. It required a three-day ride on the Union Pacific Railroad. They would not be able to travel in the same car or class, but Ch'eng-yu solved that problem by finding six other couples to accompany them. He was not the only Chinese man in San Francisco who longed for an American wife. Jennie would have her escort, and he would have his bride.

En route, the wedding party stopped to take a photograph. They preserved proof of their high spirits for posterity by swapping the men's derbies and caps for the women's bonnets for the camera. In Evanston, the "Las Vegas of the Old West," the turn-around time for a certificate of marriage was just twenty-four hours. The couples witnessed each other's unions on May 29. Reverend Leander C. Hills of the Presbyterian Church certified that the marriage was legal under Wyoming law. In the eyes of the United States, however, Jennie lost her American citizenship by marrying Ch'eng-yu—she was now considered to be Chinese. Federal law would not permit her to reclaim her American citizenship until 1932.

My grandparents lived together between two continents for nearly thirty years. They returned to San Francisco after their marriage, living for a while on the outskirts of Chinatown, where my aunt Blossom was born. Then, in 1911, my grandfather's dream of a new republic in China was realized after Dr. Sun and his followers overthrew five thousand years of the Qing Dynasty. Ch'eng-yu took his "American princess" and their three-year-old daughter to Shanghai, where he served as China's first senator from Hupei Province to the new Republic of China.

Over the next two decades, Ch'eng-yu would witness the deterioration of his beloved republic during the Warlord Era. He would be present at the death of Dr. Sun from cancer in 1925, and a supporter of the Kuomintang in the subsequent rise of Chiang Kai-shek. He and Jennie would produce three more children, of whom their first son was my father.

It had taken an earthquake to bring my grandparents together. It took a war to pull them apart. When Japan invaded China in the thirties, Ch'eng-yu sent Jennie and the children back to America while he retreated to Chungking, still working for the Nationalist government. After the Communist takeover in 1949, the family in the United States lost track of him.

Ten years ago, I had a friend search the Kuomintang archives in Taipei, and we learned that my grandfather had died in Wuchang in 1953. We may never know the cause of his death. Jennie survived him by twenty years. She lived with her younger daughter in Hollywood Hills until her death. She never remarried.

Aimee Liu, a native of Connecticut, received her B.A. from Yale University in 1975 and her MFA from Bennington College in 2006. She is the author of several books, including *Cloud Mountain* (Warner Books 1997), a novel based on the true story of her American grandmother and Chinese revolutionary grandfather. Liu's articles, essays, and short stories have appeared in various anthologies, and periodicals such as *Cosmopolitan*, *Self*, *Glamour*, and *Good Housekeeping*. She lives in Los Angeles with her husband and two sons.

The original version of this essay appeared in the *Los Angeles Times*. Reprinted with permission.

"Honor, Courage, and Commitment"

The Saving of NASCAR'S Jack Roush

By Brenda Warneka

The small open-cockpit Air-Cam lifted off the end of the runway at the Troy Municipal Airport in Troy, Alabama, banked to the left, and flew along the shore of Palos Verdes Lake. The pilot undoubtedly enjoyed the view of the community of homes clustered around the tranquil body of water below. Set in the middle of scenic woodlands, the private man-made lake is about a mile long and ranges from three feet deep at one end to thirty feet deep at the other. High-tension power lines on each side of the lake, partially obscured by trees, were hard to detect in the early evening light.

Without warning, disaster struck, as the twin-engine plane collided with steel cable support wires for the power line towers. It plunged upside down toward the lake, crashing into water that was about eight feet deep. The plane was mostly submerged as it settled in place.

Friday night, April 19, 2002, Larry and Donna Hicks were preparing to watch the six o' clock news in their lakeside home at Palos Verdes Estates outside Troy. Larry, a fifty-two-year-old retired Sergeant Major with the Marines, worked as a conservation enforcement officer for the state of Alabama, and was in the last three weeks of studying for his Master's Degree in Law Enforcement at Troy State University. He had arrived home from work half an hour earlier, and he and Donna had talked about going to a movie, but decided against it.

The TV news was just starting when they looked out the window and saw a small plane flying down the shoreline of the lake. Donna commented on how pretty it was.

"I wonder if he knows about the power lines," Larry said, just as the aircraft suddenly shuddered to a halt, flipped over, and dropped eighty to a hundred feet straight down into the lake. Larry was already running out the back door, his heart racing, as the plane hit the water, yelling behind to his wife, "Call 911! I'm going to see if I can help the pilot."

Fortunately, Larry's brother, Wayne, had left a fourteen-foot aluminum johnboat with an electric trolling motor at the lake in preparation for bass fishing that day, then hadn't shown up. The boat was charged, with everything hooked up, ready to go. Donna made the call to 911, and ran outside in time to see Larry commandeering the johnboat headed toward the Air-Cam, which was about a hundred yards offshore.

When Larry was stationed at the Marine Corps Air Station in Iwakuni, Japan, in 1984, he had spent two-and-a-half months, part time, in an intense Search and Rescue program. A Major Stone, who ran the SAR team, got him into it because he thought Larry would be good at Search and Rescue since he was muscular and a body builder. The training was specifically directed toward saving pilots who had gone down in water in fixed-wing or rotary-wing planes. Larry had learned how to get pilots out from under canopies and helicopters, and out of planes that had crashed upside down. After the training, Major Stone asked Headquarters to transfer Larry to the SAR team, but the telecommunications unit could not spare him. He had never had the opportunity to use his specialized training.

The engines of the Air-Cam were hot when it hit the lake, and the airplane was smoking in the water. High octane aviation fuel from a ruptured tank floated on the surface in greasy patterns. The back half of the aircraft and a broken wing were sticking up from the water. Larry climbed out of the boat onto the wing and tethered a line to the plane to keep the boat from floating away.

The harsh smell of gasoline assaulted his nostrils as Larry turned and shouted at his wife. "Donna! No matter what happens, I love you!"

Donna managed a puzzled "What?" before she, too, smelled the gas. It was only later that Larry thought about the danger of the plane blowing up.

The water was murky from mud kicked up when the plane hit the bottom of the lake, and Larry had trouble getting his bearings underwater. The plane had crashed into the middle of an underwater "stump field," but luckily had missed hitting any trees. The first time down, Larry felt only an empty seat and thought the pilot might have been thrown out of the plane. Running out of air, he was forced to come back to the surface. It occurred to him that maybe the plane was a two-seater.

The second time down, just as he started to push off to go back up, he felt the back of a man's neck under his hand. The pilot was hanging upside down, still strapped into his harness. Larry thought *Okay, now I know where he is.* Then his SAR training kicked in. He came back to the surface, took a deep breath, and went down for the third time.

When Larry first saw him, the pilot's face was so badly swollen that his features were almost non-existent. The doctor later said this might have been because he was upside down and had a closed-head injury.

Larry's military training—the repeat drill of what to do until it became second nature—took over: Locate pilot, extract pilot. He felt for the pilot's seatbelt; fortunately, it was one he recognized by feel from his training in the military. He released the belt and the pilot floated into his arms. Larry swam to the surface, pulling the man with him. The pilot had bones sticking out through his legs and his feet were turned the wrong way. The man was bleeding through the nose and mouth, and was no longer breathing; he had drowned.

The Troy police had arrived on the lake bank by now. Larry yelled to the officers, "He's not breathing!" and he heard one police officer say to another, "He's dead."

Larry hauled the man up against the airplane wing that was sticking up above the water, put a modified Heimlich maneuver under his ribs, pulled up to get the water out of his lungs, and then started CPR. The inert figure coughed up water and blood, and on the fifth breath he started to breathe.

"I've got him breathing again!" Larry yelled to the rescue unit on the shore.

He gripped the wing of the plane with his left hand, lying on his back in the water, supporting the pilot on his chest with his right arm to keep his head above water. He was in the lake like that for about fifteen minutes, waiting for help to arrive. The first five minutes, he felt a stinging sensation from the aviation fuel; the next five minutes were worse. At the end, he was in great pain. He found out later that the top layer of his skin had burned off.

The rescue unit brought out an extra boat, put the pilot on the backboard and floated him to shore; Larry warned them that the man was too badly injured to put him in the boat. The four members of the rescue team walked out of the lake. Larry made it as far as the bank when his legs gave way. A recovering cancer victim, he had been taking shots to boost his energy, but a policeman had to help him out of the water. It was at that point that an emergency medical technician told him that the pilot was Jack Roush.

"Who is Jack Roush?" Larry asked. The police officer and the EMT laughed.

Larry and the pilot were transported in different ambulances to Edge Regional Medical Center about four miles away. Upon arrival at the hospital, the doctors induced a coma in the pilot.

When Dr. Mark Griffin questioned Larry about how he was, he immediately asked the doctor, "How's the other guy?" The doctor told him that the pilot was probably not going to make it. Some time later, while Larry was being treated for gasoline burns on his upper body, he heard the helicopters arrive to airlift the pilot to the University of Alabama Medical Center in Birmingham, where he was put on a respirator with a trauma team working on him. After a decontamination shower, Larry was released from the hospital.

Larry and Donna (who had been waiting for him at the hospital) headed home. They were shocked upon arriving at their gated community to find news crews waiting outside the gate for a chance to interview the police, who were still trying to get the plane out of the lake, and would not allow the media inside.

Word was out, even while the rescue was taking place, that a light plane had crashed, piloted by celebrity Jack Roush, NASCAR and Winston Cup car owner since 1988, and CEO of Roush Industries, Inc., an engineering and prototype development company in Livonia, Michigan.

Earlier that day, Roush, an aircraft aficionado, had piloted his World War II vintage P-51 Mustang airplane from his Michigan home to Troy, where he was meeting friends to celebrate his sixtieth birthday. As a birthday present, the friends had arranged for Roush to fly the Air-Cam, a specialized aircraft built specifically for photography, and known for its use by *National Geographic*.

When Donna called their adult son, Brian, to tell him what had happened, she told him the name of the pilot was something like Rice or Reese or Roush, but that they did not know for sure. Brian's reaction was immediate: "Jack Roush of *NASCAR*? Are you kidding? What planet have you been living on?"

Four hours after the accident, as he tried to relax at home, Larry said to Donna in amazement, "Did what I think happened, just happen?" He stayed up all night, unable to sleep from the after-effects of so much adrenaline pumping though his body. He watched the sunrise from his patio, finally falling asleep about 4:00 p.m. the following day.

For his part, Roush was in poor condition. He had inhaled water and gasoline and had suffered closed-head injuries, rib fractures, a collapsed lung, compound fractures to his left leg, and broken ankles. He had been knocked out by a head injury when he hit the power lines, and did not remember anything from the time of the accident until he woke up in the hospital that weekend, including having gone through the drowning experience.

Six days after the accident, amazingly enough, Roush was running his business by telephone from his hospital bed. By that Sunday, he was ready for a reunion with his rescuer. He arranged for Larry and Donna to be flown by private jet to Birmingham, Alabama, where they visited him at the hospital. They walked into a room full of Jack's family and friends, who were wearing "Roush" jackets and shirts.

By now, Larry and Donna were beginning to understand the celebrity status of Jack Roush, if for no other reason than the number of telephone calls they were receiving at their home from the news media, eager to interview Larry about his heroic rescue of the man. As Larry said later, "We must have been the only people in Alabama who didn't follow NASCAR."

When Larry and Jack looked at each other for the first time after the rescue, they hugged, and Jack said "Thank you," but they were too choked up with tears and too overcome with emotion to say more. Donna and Jack's wife, Pauline, were also present and started to cry. Others in the hospital room, which included Jack Jr., one of Jack's daughters and her husband, and Jack's brother, Frank, choked up, too. It seemed a good twenty minutes before everyone recovered enough to hold a normal conversation. It was then clear from what Jack said that he was humbled by his good luck in having Larry Hicks nearby when the Air-Cam went down.

Six weeks later, Roush piloted a plane from his Michigan home and hobbled around on crutches at Dover International Speedway in Dover, Delaware, overseeing his four-car Winston Cup team. Larry and Donna were by his side.

Larry Hicks has no doubt that a higher power was at work in Jack Roush's incredible rescue. He says he did not save him; he was just the instrument. If the Air-Cam had hit the high-tension power lines instead of the support wires, the plane would have gone down in flames. If it had crashed on the ground or hit a tree in the underwater stump field where it landed, Roush undoubtedly would have been killed instantly.

If Larry and Donna had purchased the home they originally tried to buy on the other side of Palos Verdes Lake, or Larry had been late in coming home from work that day, or he and Donna had decided to go to a movie as they had discussed, or simply been in another part of the house, they would not have seen the plane go down, and the only headline would have been that Jack Roush had died in a plane crash.

If the accident had taken place a few months earlier, Larry, who had suffered a tremendous weight loss from the effects of chemotherapy and radiation treatment for nose and throat cancer, would not have been strong enough to pull Roush out of the water. If Wayne Hicks had not left the johnboat ready to go, the ending might still have been different.

But, most amazing of all, Larry was one of a small percentage of the populace with the specialized knowledge necessary to save a pilot in an upside down plane from a watery grave—specialized knowledge without which there is no question but that Jack Roush would have died. And, one other thing was necessary to save Jack's life, which is that Larry is the kind of man he is: a man of action who, even with his own less than perfect health, did not hesitate to put himself at risk to save a stranger's life.

Larry Hicks finds it hard to understand the recognition and accolades that have come his way as a result of his heroic rescue of Jack Roush. He says that as a Marine, he did not have the option of doing nothing. Among the many honors awarded him are the Marine Corps Medal of Heroism, the Alabama Attorney General's Law Enforcement Officer of the Year Award for the Southern District of Alabama, the Carnegie Award for Heroism from the Carnegie Foundation, the Kiwanis International Robert P. Connally Medal for Heroism, the Society of the Sons of the American Revolution Medal for Heroism, and the Alabama Legislative Law Enforcement Medal of Honor. The story of the rescue appeared in *People* magazine twice, and Larry and Jack were on the cover of the December 2002 issue of *NASCAR Illustrated,* and other NASCAR issues in the months that followed.

Hicks and Roush have become close friends, likening their relationship to that of brothers. They both remain very emotional about the rescue. Jack says he is now "a kinder, gentler, more humorous Jack Roush," and that his greatest fear is that he won't be able to live up to the responsibility of being "given these extra days."

Larry is proud that he lived up to the United States Marine Corps Code of serving his country with "honor, courage, and commitment," with selfless service. The Marine Code applies to both active duty marines and those who have retired or otherwise returned to civilian life. Larry says that other than his marriage to Donna and the birth of his children and grandchildren, this is the most special thing that has happened in his life. He is now making plans to learn to fly.

Go Home

By Jennie L. Phipps

There's a divinity that shapes our ends, rough-hew them how we will.

William Shakespeare

The day Grandma died was my eighth birthday. My best gift was a game board with numbers and letters printed on it. It was rough—handmade and hand-painted, with a pointer mounted on castors, which was used to spell out messages from "spirits." There was no card, and the wrappings looked used. When no one owned up to giving it to me, Mama grabbed it off the dining room table and threw it into the trash.

"It's superstitious nonsense—that silly spirit board. Devil worship," she had said. "It's not for you."

I fished it out of the trashcan after dinner when she wasn't looking. It was mine, and I wanted it.

I thought Grandma didn't know it was my birthday. She had been curled up in her big oak bed since Christmas. The cancer started on her face and shoulders where years of farm work had left her skin mottled and wrinkled. In December, the doctor told Mama that he could order chemotherapy, but it would not help. In the end, she would still die a painful death.

"No, we'll take her home and let her die in her own bed," Mama said.

So we spent the winter and part of the spring at Grandma's house in West Virginia, watching her waste away. At first, Grandma spent part of the day in a wooden rocker with a ragged cushion, telling me stories and braiding my hair. Toward the end of May she stopped getting out of bed, and from the kitchen we could hear her moaning and talking to herself. As the summer wore on, Grandma forgot who I was.

"Sister, have you fed the chickens?" she would say to me. "How many times do I have to ask you to feed the chickens?"

"Grandma, there are no chickens, and I'm not Sister."

"Sister, don't argue. Do what I tell you."

Air doesn't move in a dying person's room. Even the breeze would rather be someplace else.

"You sit there and watch her," Mama ordered. "If she needs me, call."

Grandma gasped for breath, shuddering and rasping. I rocked back and forth in the rocking chair beside her bed, praying to God and Grandma, "Don't let me be sitting here by myself when it happens."

It was especially stifling after my birthday party. While Mama was cleaning up, I was watching Grandma. She stirred a little and opened her eyes.

"Sister, did you get my present?" She stared at me. "It was for you."

"What present?"

"You know. Your birthday present. I love you, Sister. Now, go home."

Grandma sank back, her jaw going slack and her mouth falling open.

"Mama! Quick! Hurry, Mama! *Mama!*"

As soon as Mama came, I ran to my room, which was directly above Grandma's room. The cicadas crying in the pear tree outside and the sound of Mama crying in Grandma's room below made me sick.

I picked up my spirit board and balanced it lightly on my knees. Tuning out everything, I listened only to the noises in my head while my fingers spelled the words *GO HOME. GO HOME. GO HOME.*

The burial was over in short order, and now I could hear voices from the room below as Mama divided up Grandma's possessions.

"It was a blessing. She was in such pain."

"Thank God she didn't know anything or anybody at the end."

"She was a good woman. She worked so hard all of her life."

Through it all, the spirit board kept telling me *GO HOME, GO HOME, GO HOME.*

"We'll go when we can," Mama was telling someone. "This kind of business takes time."

But the spirit board didn't listen. *GO HOME.*

"I thought I threw that thing away." Mama appeared at my door as the message came through one more time. "You're too old and too smart for that kind of trash. Get rid of it!"

"No!"

"Don't be smart with me, young lady. You're being disrespectful. Your grandmother would never have put up with it. Now let me have that thing."

"No. It's mine. Grandma gave it to me."

"Your grandmother did no such thing, but I don't have time to argue with you. Just throw it away, and we'll forget this happened."

"I want to go home! I want to leave here," I sobbed.

"Tomorrow," Mama said. "We're going tomorrow. But don't try to bring that thing, or I'll give you something to cry about!"

The spirit board was adamant: *GO HOME.*

I loaded my things into the car and when Mama wasn't looking, I stuffed "Spirit" out of sight under the back of the driver's seat. It was nearly noon when we left. The car swayed around the mountains. The spirit board slipped out from under its hiding place. I dived to get it.

"Don't kick the back of my seat," Mama warned me. "You're too old for that."

It was rainy, and the roads were slick. Mama didn't even turn around as she yelled at me. I rested the board on my knees and waited for the message, *GO HOME.*

Mama glanced back at me in the rearview mirror and frowned. "I'm putting an end to this once and for all. Spirit boards are for pagan, stupid people." Mama reached behind her, grabbed the board and heaved it out the car window. It landed in somebody's cornfield. I watched through the back window, trying to count the rows.

Mama's neck was red. "We usually stop and get ice cream, but today, after this spirit board business, I don't think that's a good idea. We're going straight home. No stops, no treats."

She aimed the car across the bridge over the Ohio River. The four o'clock whistle blew, announcing shift change as we passed. Not stopping for ice cream kept us ahead of the coal mine traffic, which usually meant the cars on the bridge were bumper to bumper. Today, we were practically alone.

"I'll bet you're hungry," Mama said, a few miles past the bridge. "We would have stopped if you hadn't insisted on bringing that stupid board. Now you'll just have to wait."

"Grandma gave me the spirit board," I mumbled. "She wanted me to have it."

The car veered onto the shoulder as Mama turned around enough to slap my face.

I didn't cry. I just wanted to go home.

Mama sighed. "I'm sorry, but you try my patience. Maybe I should stop and get a cup of coffee. I didn't mean to hurt you."

"I want to go home," I whispered.

We stopped at a little roadside cafe. The owner had the radio on. The announcer was giving the horrendous details. Some people were crying. The bridge over the Ohio River had collapsed only minutes after we'd crossed it. Cars bumper to bumper at shift change all fell into the river, sliding unstoppable into the deep, churning water - eighty-eight vehicles and one hundred and twenty dead bodies, only two survivors.

Mama prayed for the dead. I prayed for Grandma and my spirit board.

Jennie L. Phipps is a business writer who specializes in media, small business, and health. She is a regular contributor to *Newsweek Japan, Television Week, Bankrate.com, Industry Week*, and *Investor's Business Daily*, as well as *Health Scout News* and *Modern Physician*. Jennie is passionate about old houses and writes about them for *Old House Journal, Preservation Online*, and *Smart Homeowner*. She also publishes a subscription newsletter for
professional non-fiction writers called "Freelance Success."
www.freelancesuccess.com.

Fate Has a Name

By Ann Newton Holmes

Zenobia walked into my writing class in January 1990. I had been waiting for her for nearly thirty years

When I first encountered the name Zenobia in the early sixties, the roots of my hair tingled. The name whispered to me of exotic and mysterious connections, of things unknowable, of unexpected events. I became entranced with Zenobia, the proud and beautiful Queen of Palmyra who tangled with Rome in 272 AD, after reading about her in the 1953 edition of the *Columbia-Viking Desk Encyclopedia* I had inherited from my grandmother. I was looking up the Roman emperor Zeno, and Zenobia followed Zeno.

At seventies costume parties, I was a regal Zenobia in flowing caftan and towering peacock feather headdress. Then, in the late eighties, I started writing a historical novel set in sixteenth century India. How could I name the antagonist, the sinuous and seductive concubine, anything other than Zenobia?

The real live Zenobia wore a brown sweater and a tweed skirt. She wasn't the Zenobia of my fantasies, nor did she seem weighted with portent, but my scalp tingled nonetheless. I skipped an appointment to introduce myself to my fellow student after class.

Zenobia had just moved to Napa Valley and wanted to link up with other writers. As we talked, I discovered that she, too, was involved with India; she had written a book on the Hindu god Shiva.

I mentioned that my husband, Fred, and I were to depart for India in three weeks to do research for my novel.

"Will you pass through Jodhpur?" Zenobia asked.

Jodhpur was our destination.

"Do you know of the hotel, the Ajit Bhawan?"

Tingles turned to chills. Out of the huge Indian subcontinent of nearly a billion people, she had named the exact hotel where, on the guidebook's recommendation, we had booked a room.

Zenobia explained that the previous year, while she completed her research for her book on Shiva, she had lived at the Ajit Bhawan for three months. The owners, Maharaj Swaroop Singh, the "uncle" of the Maharaja of Jodhpur, and his wife, Rani Usha Devi, had become friends.

"Will you take them a gift from me?" she asked.

"Of course," was all I could say.

At the Ajit Bhawan, a small twentieth-century palace with idiosyncratic stone cottages scattered about a large garden, Fred and I showered off the dust of desert travel and sent our business card to the owners. On the back of the card, we mentioned that we had brought them a gift from Zenobia. An hour later, a tall young man in a huge red turban arrived at our door with an invitation to afternoon tea on the verandah of their private quarters. The same young man returned to lead us through the garden into the palace where Swaroop and Usha Devi received us.

Usha Devi was an exotic beauty of my own age. To my thinking, she should have been named Zenobia. Swaroop, a few years older, was dashing, from his traditional turban to the turned-up toes of his *jooties*. Zenobia's lovely gift basket of expensive toiletries, not available in Jodpur in 1990, made a big hit.

Talk of Zenobia soon turned to our years of travel and research in India, Fred's expertise in Hindu temples, and my historical novel about a princess who was an ancestral relation of Swaroop. That evening, they asked us to share their table at dinner.

Two days later, Swaroop invited us to join them for the wedding of a noble's daughter in a nearby village. He thought it would be a grand opportunity for me to experience old customs in action. "The Maharaja will be there, and, where he is, traditions are practiced," he explained.

Indian wedding ceremonies are scheduled at the hour astrologers deem auspicious. This ceremony was set for 2:00 am, but we entered the bride's house about 10:00 the evening before. Swaroop led Fred and me to where the men gathered in a large reception room with straight-backed chairs lined up around the walls. The men wore impeccable turbans and brilliant white kurta pajamas. As waiters passed silver trays of whiskey and cigarettes, Swaroop introduced us to much of the aristocracy of Rajasthan. Over and over, I silently thanked Zenobia for this opportunity to meet the people I needed to know for my research.

After an hour, a servant delivered me to Usha Devi who, with the other silken and bejeweled women, lounged on white muslin-covered mattresses under the stars. When the Maharani and the Queen Mother of Jodhpur made their entrance, noble women dropped rupees at their feet and touched their toes. Then the red-garbed bride bowed before them to receive their royal blessing, and women of the bride's family decorously danced for us, the bells on their ankles marking the beat.

Sometime after midnight, trumpets and drums sounded in the distance. They grew louder and louder as the *barat*, the noisy procession of the men of the groom's party, made its slow progression through the narrow, dusty streets of the village, led by the groom mounted on a white horse.

Fred remained with the men, and Swaroop introduced him to the Maharaja of Jodhpur when he arrived. They struck up a conversation about the Maharaja's huge Art Deco palace, the Umaid Bhawan, that he called his "white elephant." People criticized it, he said, as British Civic Monolithic, because a British architect designed it, or as Moghul, because of its prominent domes. Fred, drawing upon his knowledge of Hindu temples, explained it was neither, but rather a traditional Hindu temple-mountain palace, reminiscent of Angkor Wat in Cambodia.

The wedding was the beginning of a friendship and collaboration with the Maharaja of Jodhpur that allowed Fred and me to use our Indian expertise in new ways. He commissioned us to write the text and take the photographs for a fiftieth anniversary coffee table book about the Umaid Bhawan Palace, and we continue to work with him and his Museum Trust on other major projects. Our friendship with Swaroop lasted until his untimely death in 2003, and continues with his wife Usha Devi to this day.

Ironically, when I returned to Napa Valley eleven weeks after I had initially met Zenobia, she had disappeared. I tried to track her down, but found not a trace. After thirty years of fascination with her name, Zenobia came into my life and propelled my husband and me on a collision course with Jodhpur royalty that fulfilled our fondest dreams—then vanished.

Fate has a name: Zenobia.

Ann Newton Holmes lives on a hillside overlooking Napa Valley in California. Her latest coffee table book on Hindu architecture and mythology, *Jodhpur's Umaid Bhawan, the Maharaja of Palaces*, was published in India in August 2008. Ann has published articles on India in

The Christian Science Monitor, *Jetwings* and *The World & I.* She has written two novels set in Rajasthan, and her short stories, rooted in India, as well as in a childhood spent fishing the West with her nomadic parents, have appeared in *New Frontiers*, *Grit*, *ArtScan*, *Cup of Comfort*, and *More than Wine*.

When Denise Created Barney

By Alaina Smith

Luck is the residue of opportunity and design.
Branch Rickey
General Manager, Brooklyn Dodgers

Fate had a way of watching out for Denise.

In high school, after the boyfriend she thought was "The One" moved to Brazil, a crushed and despondent Denise caught sight of another young man who looked strikingly similar to her lost love. The resemblance drew her to this new man, and soon surrogate interest became genuine love. While still a teenager, she married the man and gave birth to a cherished daughter.

As Denise became an adult, fate would continue to have things to say about how her life would proceed. One day while driving, she was first in line at a stoplight. She waited for the light to turn green, but when it did, Denise didn't pull forward. She sat there, but not because she was busy applying lipstick or rifling through her purse. She sat at the green light because something in her mind said "Don't go." Seconds later, a car came barreling through the intersection, running its red light, zooming directly into the spot where Denise would have been had she obeyed the traffic signal.

Events like these had happened throughout her life, but none was more fateful than that spring day in 1982 when Denise created Barney.

At age thirty-five, Denise was in the process of a divorce, living alone, and caring for her nine-year-old daughter. She found work at a community college bookstore. Although she enjoyed interacting with the students and staff, there was one student, at least ten years her junior, who relentlessly pursued dating her. Denise wasn't interested. Her divorce wasn't yet final, and she wasn't ready to date anyone. Besides, she knew this man was not for her, but he refused to take no for an answer.

"I need to invent a boyfriend," Denise said to her boss, Dee. "Then maybe he'll leave me alone. I can be talking to you about my boyfriend when he comes in, and maybe he'll finally get the hint."

"Sounds good," Dee agreed. "What's his name going to be?"

"He should have a big, tough, biker-type name," Denise said. "Spike or Butch or something."

She thought about it some more and realized she needed something not quite so stereotypical, but still manly. She decided on Barney. That would work.

"So what's Barney going to be like?" Dee asked.

Denise reflected on what type of person she would like. She thought about what she'd learned from her marriage, and she considered what she wanted now, at this stage of her life. Although she felt certain she'd never choose to get married again, she was able to picture an ideal mate.

Denise thoughtfully described Barney. "Well, to start with, he'll be a happy person. He'll be healthy, he'll have a good relationship with his mom and his family, and he'll come with no baggage—no ex-wife, no kids. He'll be six feet tall and have blue eyes. He won't smoke. He'll be handy, able to fix things, and he'll be self-sufficient. He'll cook and clean for himself, and whatever his job is, it'll be a job he can leave at work and not bring home with him."

Denise was lost in thought, dreaming up her perfect man. The more she thought about him, the more she became uncertain about the name. "Maybe instead, I should give him a sophisticated name," she said to Dee. "Like Michael or Geoffrey with a G, or—Richard. Yes, Richard."

So Barney became Richard, and the next time Denise's young suitor came into the bookstore, she put her plan into action. She talked about how wonderful Richard was, going on and on about this wonderful man who made her so happy. Eventually, the student got the hint. His determination fizzled and he gave up on Denise. "Richard" had served his purpose.

Three months later in June, the divorce became final. With that sense of closure, she was finally feeling like she would be open to new possibilities—and fate agreed.

It was a Tuesday morning, six days after Denise was officially a single woman again. One of the college instructors who had become a friend, Bob, came into the bookstore. He was accompanied by his brother, who was visiting from out of state.

"This is my brother, Dick," Bob said. "He works on the Goodyear Blimp."

"Hi," the man said, smiling at Denise. "My name's Barney."

Barney pulled from his pocket a small rubber eraser shaped like the Goodyear Blimp and handed it to Denise. "Here's a seed," he said, his eyes twinkling. "Grow your own."

Denise squeezed the eraser in her hands and looked up at him. Barney's smile was dazzling and constant. Denise was immediately smitten with the tall, blue-eyed man.

She introduced herself, and they talked a bit longer; then it was time for Bob and Barney to go. As Barney walked out of the bookstore, Denise did something impetuous and out of character. "Call me if you want to go out!" she exclaimed.

She was instantly mortified at her boldness, but Barney didn't seem to mind. He looked back, grinning, and said "Okay."

Later, Denise asked Bob about his brother. "What is his name?" she asked. "You introduced him as Dick, but he said his name is Barney."

"Barney's his nickname," Bob explained. "He goes by Barney at work and with friends. His real name is Richard, so the family calls him Dick."

Barney … Richard … was it only a naming coincidence, or was it possible Denise's perfect man had come to life? Whether or not it was true, he had left an electric first impression on her. She was infatuated. Fortunately, when she returned to work the next day, Dee approached her with good news.

"Bob's brother came by yesterday afternoon and left his card for you," Dee said, handing her a business card. Denise held the card in her hands. It was a classy card, with a silver embossed Goodyear Blimp and contact information for the base located in Southern California. It read: *Richard K. "Barney" Spielman, Senior Airship Mechanic.*

Denise put the card in her pocket, pulling it out periodically throughout the afternoon to admire it.

That day after work, Denise drove to her best friend's house to show her the card. "It's the coolest card," Denise said to Pat, pulling it out.

"Did you call him?" Pat asked.

"No, I can't. There's no local number on it."

"Give me that," Pat said, taking the card and flipping it over. There, on the back, was Barney's hotel phone number.

"You have to turn it over," Pat counseled. "When men want you to call them, they write their private numbers on the back."

Denise's eyes widened. She grabbed the card and sprinted to Pat's telephone. Barney wasn't there when she called, so she left a message. Eagerly hoping to hear back, Denise had no idea that by then, Barney had already called every "D. Smith" in the phone book looking for her, not knowing she had an unlisted number.

When he returned her call that same night, he asked her if she'd like to go for coffee.

"I'll go out for hot chocolate," Denise said, "but I don't drink coffee." Barney admitted he didn't drink coffee, either. The two planned to meet during Denise's break from work the next day, Thursday, at the college snack bar.

Thursday morning before her date, Denise grilled Bob about his brother and found out that Barney had never been married, nor did he have children. Later, at the snack bar with Barney, Denise found out more about him. He was already sounding great, but the clincher was when she discovered that they both loved to play Scrabble.

"Nobody beats me at Scrabble," Denise bragged.

"I'll beat you at Scrabble," Barney quietly assured her, smiling.

Denise offered to show him around town the next day, and he said he'd like that. She didn't know that he had to take the day off work to do so, but he did, happily.

As they drove through the Columbia River Gorge that morning, on their way to Multnomah Falls, Barney reminded her that the falls had a left-side exit, so she should get in the left lane. Denise looked at him, shocked. How did he know? It turned out that Barney was an Oregonian, like Denise, only temporarily transplanted to California. He didn't need to be shown around town; he just wanted to spend time with her.

At Multnomah Falls, Denise asked Barney about himself. With each sentence, he provided the puzzle pieces that snapped together to fit her dream of the perfect mate. He didn't smoke, and his behavior was that of a cheerful, confident man. He was close to his widowed mother, for whom he had great love and respect. He enjoyed a warm relationship with his siblings and shared a goofy camaraderie with his brother, Bob. He was a family man by nature, but one who had not yet created a family of his own.

After their morning at Multnomah Falls, Denise and Barney decided to play Scrabble at Rooster Rock State Park. They sat on the grass, and as Denise pulled out the Scrabble game she'd brought, Barney pulled wine from a cooler. Denise had a glass and relaxed on the grass. They drew tiles to see who would go first, and Barney won. He selected his tiles from the bag, and then promptly played all seven tiles on his first turn, spelling P-U-R-S-U-I-T.

Denise was stunned. Barney could play after all. A lot of wine and tiles later, Denise—a small woman with a low tolerance for alcohol—found herself too giggly and tipsy to finish the game. Barney would have to beat her another day, and he did.

Six months later, Barney proposed marriage. Although they'd seen each other only sporadically during his travels with the Goodyear Blimp, the couple talked every day, sometimes twice a day. Denise knew he was the man for her. Through their talks and time together, she had learned he was an inherently happy person, self-sufficient, able to fix almost anything, and an excellent cook. In fact, without exception, every trait Denise had assigned to her imaginary Barney/Richard was alive in this very real man. The couple was married one year from the day they met.

Today, Denise is infinitely grateful for the young student—her unwanted suitor—who forced her to really think about what she wanted in a mate. Because of him, Denise brought Barney to life in her mind one spring day and shared him with the world. Three months later, when she was emotionally ready to move on, and her divorce was final, Barney appeared. Denise still marvels not only at the fact that Fate had given her a perfect mate, just as she had designed him, but that she met him well after the day she "invented" him, at the point in her life when she was finally ready to open her heart again. California-based Barney arrived at the right place, an Oregon bookstore, at exactly the right time. Married for twenty-five years now, Denise and Barney are still happily coupled, and Barney is still beating her—frequently—at Scrabble.

Alaina Smith is a writer whose short inspirational stories have appeared in multiple volumes of two book series, *Chocolate For Women* and *A Cup of Comfort.* She writes both fiction and nonfiction and enjoys lending her editing skills to anyone in need. She also works as an office administrator for a wilderness conservation organization. Alaina and her husband, Frank, live near Portland, Oregon, only a few miles away from Alaina's mom and stepdad ... Denise and Barney.

Jacob! Jacob!
Reborn September 11, 2001

By Arlene Uslander

Jacob Herbst was not unfamiliar with the sight of death and destruction. Living in Israel from the time he was three years old, he had seen much fighting and killing. As a young man, Jacob had fought in wars, but he had never been so close to dying as he was on September 11, 2001. What he saw on television that day was something he never imagined he would see in his lifetime. The fact that his own life almost ended that day, but because of some strange "touch of fate" it did not, is a thought he will carry with him for the rest of his days; "a thought that still brings moisture" to his eyes.

A computer engineer by trade, Jacob is founder and CEO of FilesX, a software development company located in Boston. Although he lives in Israel, Jacob travels to the United States frequently on business. He arrived in Boston on September 9th. On the evening of September 10th, he met with his good friend and business consultant Steve Duplessie, founder and Senior Analyst of Enterprise Storage Group, a consulting and marketing firm located in Milford, thirty miles west of Boston. The purpose of the visit was to do some brainstorming about the direction of FilesX, and the hiring of a vice president of sales.

"We didn't come up with the names of any candidates who sounded like they would fill the bill," said Jacob, "so I thanked Steve very much, said we would talk further, and I bid him good night."

ESG is housed on the top floor of a small two-story building, and as Jacob walked through the parking lot, he heard his name being called: "Jacob! Jacob!"

Jacob turned and saw Steve waving at him to come back upstairs, which he did. Steve told Jacob that he had thought of someone who might be just the person for vice president of sales. His name was Michael Beaudet. Steve called Michael while Jacob was there, suggested that Michael might want to interview with Jacob, and said that Jacob would be in touch with him.

Jacob's time was already scheduled for the rest of the evening, and he was leaving Boston the next morning for Los Angeles, where he would visit with friends before going on to the Silicon Valley for business. After he left Steve, he thought to himself, *Ah, should I call Michael tonight or should I not?*

"But" recalled Jacob, "something told me I should call, so I left a message on Michael's voice mail, asking if we could meet later that evening. Michael called me back while I was at a dinner meeting and said, 'I can't meet you tonight, but I can meet you very early tomorrow morning,' so we scheduled our meeting for 6:00 a.m."

The flight Jacob was scheduled to take the following morning was due to depart from Boston's Logan Airport at 8:45—American Airlines, Flight 11, to Los Angeles.

"The meeting with Michael was excellent," said Jacob, "but it took longer than I had anticipated. I barely had time to catch the flight; it is about an hour's drive from our office to the airport, but still I decided I would try to make it."

However, traffic slowed him down more than he had expected, and as Jacob was getting closer to the airport in his rental car, he realized that he had already missed his flight. He thought he would go on to the airport to try to get on the next flight. It was now about ten minutes past nine. Then, all of a sudden, he heard on the car radio that a plane had hit the World Trade Center in New York City.

"First I thought it was a sick joke," said Jacob. "You know how some people say bizarre things when they call in on radio talk shows. And then I thought that maybe it was a small private plane like the one that hit the Empire State Building a few years ago. However, they then announced that it was a passenger plane, and a few minutes later, reported that the second plane had hit; it was American Airlines, Flight 11, bound for Los Angeles. *The plane I was supposed to be on.* As you can imagine, I was in great shock!"

Jacob wondered what he should do. Should he go to the airport and try to take a later flight, or what? He decided to go back to the hotel and try to find out what was happening. The first thing he did when he got there, however, was call Michael Beaudet.

"I called to thank you, Mike," said Jacob. Mike thought Jacob was calling to thank him for the meeting.

"Do you have any idea what's going on? Look at the TV!" Michael exclaimed.

"Yes, I know what is going on, and I would like to thank you for saving my life. If you had been able to meet with me last night, I would have been on the American Airlines flight that crashed into the Twin Towers."

Jacob continued to watch what was happening on TV. "It was terrible—a horrible sight!" he said.

All the airports were shut down, so Jacob did not get back to Israel until September 15. He was able to contact his family—not by telephone because there was no phone access, but by e-mail, "which shows you," he pointed out, "how important the Internet is."

However, more important to Jacob, husband of Michaela, father of four grown children and two young grandchildren, is the lesson he learned from his close brush with death. He thinks about September 11 a lot, "and," he says, "it is still not so easy. I have learned to postpone personal plans less, especially ones I really want to make. Let's say you want to go someplace nice with your family, or spend more time with your kids, and you tend to put it off. You say, 'Oh, we can do that another time. I have business to take care of.' I realize now it is possible there might not *be* another time. Let's do it *now*. Go on a nice trip. Go with the grandkids. Tomorrow is nothing that is very secure anymore, so I am less apt to put things off. You can plan very well, but it isn't always within your control.

"The experience also helped me to put more balance into my life—to be more aware of priorities. I still put a high priority on business when needed, but I make more time for other things as well."

When he is in the United Sates at the FilesX office, Jacob sees Michael Beaudet every day, and he often thanks Michael for saving his life.

When Michael tells the story, according to Jacob, he says, "I knew when Jacob called to thank me for saving his life that fateful morning, I had gotten the job!"

"This is the first time that I have talked extensively about that day," Jacob said when interviewed for this story. "I consider that I was reborn on September 11, 2001."

Yes, it is true that Michael Beaudet had much to do with Jacob's "rebirth," because he could not meet with Jacob the night before, and the meeting went on longer than anticipated the next morning. And the traffic slowed Jacob down on his way to the airport. Yet equally responsible is Steve Duplessie, who called out through the open window, "Jacob, Jacob!" What if

Steve had not suddenly thought of Michael Beaudet for the job? Or what if Jacob had not heard Steve call him and had gone on into the night?

Arlene Uslander is the author of fifteen non-fiction books, over four hundred articles and essays, and is the recipient of numerous journalism awards. She is also a professional freelance editor. Arlene and her husband, Ira, now live in Sonora, California, after spending their lifetimes in Chicago. Besides her great love of writing, Arlene enjoys reading, music, theater, and travel. Of all her published books, this is her favorite because of the wonderful people she has come to know— the story contributors.

Fate Glistens

By Ray Duarte

Refugio Duarte, Salvador's father and Ramon's grandfather, is a gentle little brown man known to five-year-old Ramon as A*buelito,* meaning "grandfather." Refugio smiles as he sits on his favorite stool, whittling with his knife a wooden oxen for a toy carriage, just like the larger ones that could often be heard creaking up and down the graveled streets of old Los Angeles a century before.

Abuelito, in his broken English, says to Ramon: "Ramoncito, el carneeval, she comes to town tonight. I tinks we go. Ju come with us, jes?"

Ramon's eyes dazzle at what will be his toy, but tonight Ramoncito and his grandpa will hold hands as they visit and enjoy *el carneeval.*

There is the blur of lights from the distance, radiant and kaleidoscopic. In the center of the Gardens in old San Fernando, a carousel projects the joyful music of organ pipes playing delightfully with multicolored horses circling round, some fast, some slow. Much in the way life is: a cornucopia of sights and sounds. But there is only one multicolored horse that carries Ramon, who is unaware that he is filled with the magic of two worlds: the world of the secular, dark and fearful, and the world of the spirit—filled with prayer, light, and hope because of his belief and embracement of God. And because of that belief, Ramon is filled with the strength of magic to carry him between two worlds as his fate glistens towards eternity with a gleeful smile.

"Try the cotton candy, Ramoncito—it's wonderful!" Abuelito hands him a delightful stick of puffed sugar. Moments before, Ramon had watched as the sugar was heated to a liquid and spun by a metal head through holes against a bowl, and now it is consumed as an unforgettable treat, with fate's magic inducing forgetfulness of everything but his immediate existence.

Fifteen years have passed. It is Saturday morning, the sixth of February 1971. The phone rings. It is Salvador calling his only son, a son who chose to marry without his papa's blessing, something that is just not done in their cultural generation. It is unheard of. It is unthinkable.

"Hello?" Ramon answers the telephone.

"Ramon." The voice on the other end quivers, saddened and passive.

"Papa?"

Salvador sorrowfully breaks into tears; he has not spoken to Ramon since his son married out of the faith and without his blessing. Two years have passed since the wedding Salvador had refused to attend.

"Your grandfather passed away last night."

Ramon can hear his father's grief, made worse by memories of Grandmother's passing just a few years before.

"Papa, may I see you?" Ramon gently asks.

Ramon asks the question out of respect for his father, who has expressed more than once his wish not to see him again. Ramon has forgiven the pain this has caused him, but hard as he tries, he cannot forget the heartfelt devastation he feels. He will remember his feelings now as a lesson to understand the pain of his own sons later in life when a divorce is necessary. A lesson that teaches him never to disown his sons and always to forgive them, when they may not know how hurtful words can be.

Ramon enters his parents' living room. The family's good friends Mr. and Mrs. Ferra are there, visiting Salvador and Juanita to express their condolences. Ramon immediately embraces his father.

"I am so sorry, Papa."

The presence of Mr. and Mrs. Ferra, aware of the personal tragedy that had occurred two years before between Ramon and his father, helps to cement the process of healing, with Mr. Ferra verbalizing his observation of the son embracing his father.

"Now there's a true and loving son," he proclaims. "A son who knows how to comfort his own papa."

Mr. Ferra represents the elders of their community; his statement conveying immense credibility. Ramon's mother quietly weeps at the sight of healing between father and son.

The wake for Ramon's grandfather is on Monday night. The entire Duarte family has gathered for the evening Rosary. Early Tuesday morning, the Requiem Mass will be recited. Burial will follow at the San Fernando Mission Cemetery. On this dark and sad Monday night, Ramon falls into an uneasy sleep. His last conscious thought is about Abuelito, and how his grandfather's death has brought him back into the family with his papa.

"I will miss you, Abuelito," Raymond whispers in his sleep, as he dreams of the voice of a little brown man saying, "Ramoncito *el car-nee-val, she comes to town tonight, but you must not follow me!*" A distant mist embraces Grandfather as he walks away, then turns back to Ramon, and says, *"It will be all right, Ramoncito, I'll be back; you must sleep for now."*

It is one minute after six in the morning, February 9, 1971. Ramon is in the deepest level of sleep. He has been excused from his work as a nurse at the hospital today in order to attend his grandfather's funeral. At this time, Ramon would normally be arriving at work, walking beneath the "Admissions" ambulance port at Olive View Medical Center in Sylmar, near San Fernando.

Suddenly, there is a crescendo of rolling sound that most who are sleeping do not hear. Those who are awake will describe it as the sound of a huge train clanging along its tracks as it approaches closer and closer. The ground begins moving in waves, undulating in enormous surges. The entire earth rises. Ramon awakens in mid-air. The earth strikes down like a hammer, followed by intense shaking side to side.

In less than one minute, an earthquake injures over one thousand people and kills more than fifty others in the city of San Fernando. The entire east wing of the Veterans Hospital collapses, one of four hospitals totally destroyed. All communications systems are shattered. Hospitals in the area, ordered to evacuate, are sending patients to each other, not knowing that a reservoir will soon fail in their path. Freeways are smashed.

Dawn reveals a city with streets broken by geysers of water, intermingled with spires of flames. Entire facades of two- and three-story buildings have been sliced away, with furniture hanging precariously above those who walk below, in shock at what has occurred.

Blended together within the cauldrons of fire in Ramon's dreams, are images of multicolored horses that circle round, some fast, some slow, but only one filled with the magic of being in the right place at the right time, riding in the vision of that one little boy, now grown to be a man, who will awake soon to a vision of two worlds glistening towards eternity with a gleeful smile, and gentle taps on a shoulder.

During the severe ground shaking, the ambulance port at Olive View Medical Center collapses, killing those running out of the building, with the entire first floor disappearing into the ground.

Abuelito's death on the evening of February 5 saved Ramon's life. There are billions of hearts beating around the world, but Grandfather's heart as it stopped, not only brought healing to a family in pain, but also saved a life. That wonderful heart that loved beyond what words could ever say.

Ray Duarte, RN, a nephrology specialist and researcher, has been published in medical journals and has lectured at national medical conferences. One of his articles was referenced in the *New England Journal of Medicine*. After publishing thirty abstracts and nine manuscripts in his field, Ray has changed his focus from technical to creative writing. His story "Forever Smile" was published in *Chicken Soup for the Soul - Love Stories* (February 2008). He is the research expert at www.babyboomertalkradio.com.

Enjoy getting to know Ray better by visiting his website at www.rayduarte.com .

The Guide

By Mary-Alice Boulter

The air was cool, a slight breeze playing through the mist as Paul and Jack set out from Port Angeles that morning. The sun was not yet up, but it promised to be a good day for fishing.

Paul cranked over the inboard motor in the small boat. It caught after a couple of tries and emitted a healthy, throaty resonance. As Paul listened with satisfaction to the sound of the engine, Jack stashed their lunch, along with extra fuel and supplies. Their deep-water fishing gear was ready and waiting to help catch some fine salmon from the current run. The men steered the boat out of the sheltered harbor and headed around the hook into the Strait of Juan de Fuca, the body of water between Washington State and Canadian British Columbia, and west into the Pacific Ocean.

The salmon were running strong. By midday, Paul and Jack had caught and cleaned their daily limit, storing the sleek silver fish on ice in the waiting coolers. None of the fish was a record catch, but they didn't care. They had plenty of coral meat to smoke to provide many a good meal.

Using barbless hooks, the men caught and released several more fish, simply for the pleasure of the sport. They were far out in the ocean by now. A thin overcast in the sky high above them screened out the sun. The quiet expanse of sea and sky seemed to carry on endlessly as they trolled farther west, savoring the treasured shared ritual of long-time friends.

Paul, a seasoned sailor, always kept a weather eye out for changes in the sky and ocean. A storm had been forecast in the next forty-eight hours at the time they left port, but the men knew they would return that day and be home long before it struck.

As the afternoon passed pleasantly, the high mist thickened. The sun was hiding behind growing banks of low clouds filled with moisture.

"Guess we'd better pack up and head in," Paul said. "Looks like there's a good fog rolling in." They dismantled and stashed their gear and secured loose containers. Paul started the engine while Jack raised the anchor. Then Paul, steering by the onboard compass, turned northeast toward land.

They cruised at a leisurely pace, reluctant to end the day. The fog gradually closed in, wrapping them in its cool, tenuous embrace. Paul eased back on the throttle to adjust for limited visibility. They continued moving slowly ahead.

Soon the heavy mist was thick and palpable, blanketing sound. The two men could barely see the front of the sixteen-foot boat. Small waves lapped the sides. They were too far out to hear the fog horns, but Paul wasn't worried. He had used the instruments to bring him home many times before.

Paul noticed the compass needle drifting. He steered to portside to bring it back in line. It began slowly swinging to the right, and kept moving, even after Paul completed his correction and straightened the wheel. Paul tapped the compass glass. The needle veered again, then began to slowly swing from one side to the other. He frowned. He adjusted the instrument and again tapped the glass. The needle did not steady itself.

"Damn!" he muttered. "This is a heck of a time for the compass to go out." However, he wasn't too concerned. He had a good instinct for direction and was comfortable on the ocean. He knew the area. They had avoided major shipping lanes, and the running lights were working. He had a bell with a clanging tone that carried well through dense, moisture-laden air. They would be fine.

Jack noticed Paul tinkering with the compass. "What's wrong, Paul?" he asked.

"Oh, the compass is acting up. But I know where we are, and there's no real problem," Paul answered.

Jack looked a little worried. "But how can you be sure we're going in the right direction? You can't see a damn thing in this fog."

"It's okay, Jack. Land is this way. It'll take us a while to get there as slow as we're goin', but we'll get there all right."

"I think you're wrong," said Jack. "I think land is in *that* direction. We're heading farther out."

"Now don't get all heated up," Paul responded. "I know what I'm doin'. We're going in the right direction." He clanged the bell a couple of times to warn anyone who might be near their location. He repeated it several times, spacing the strokes to give the sound a chance to carry more clearly.

Jack grew more anxious. He said nothing for a few minutes, but kept peering into the fog in all directions. He wore a strained look, his mouth tight and his brow furrowed. He licked his lips. Paul could see Jack was beginning to panic, and he started to make small talk to distract his friend.

"Hey, Jack, remember that trip last summer to the Ilwaco Peninsula? Boy, that was some fish you hooked. I figured he was gonna pull you right on overboard!" He chuckled at the memory.

Jack would not be sidetracked from his concern about their present situation. He began to argue with Paul. "Look, I'm sure we're headin' in the wrong direction. Let's steer her that way."

Paul disagreed. He throttled back the engine and turned to talk with Jack.

As the men argued quietly, they did not notice a swell of movement in the water near their boat. Gently, with almost no sound, a huge sleek shape surfaced alongside the small craft. Paul glanced portside—and froze. An enormous dark eye seemed to be gazing directly into his.

"Well, I'll be damned!" he breathed. "Hush up, Jack, and turn around slowly, and look. Don't be scared."

His friend looked at him, puzzled. Then, he half-turned and glanced over his shoulder. He yelled and dove for one of the oars.

Paul grabbed Jack's arm and wrestled the oar from his grasp. "Don't be stupid. He's a heck of a lot bigger than we are. He won't hurt us if you just calm down."

"What the hell *is* it?" Jack whispered in a hoarse voice, trembling slightly.

"It's a whale," said Paul, a big smile on his face. "He's come visiting." He gazed with admiration at the huge beast hanging motionless in the water.

The whale's eye, large as Paul's closed fist, looked at them. The creature emitted a soft sigh, spraying a small fountain of droplets from its blowhole. It began to glide forward, then stopped and waited. It then moved ahead again, before stopping once more, and waiting.

Paul chuckled. "Ya know what, Jack? I think that big feller wants us to follow him."

"You're crazy!" Jack yelled. "I'm not gonna follow any damned whale!"

"Then I guess you'd better jump in and swim, 'cause this boat is following that whale. He's goin' in the right direction. He's showing us the way through the fog."

Jack began to argue again in earnest. "Hell, Paul, we'll end up lost in the Pacific Ocean! Land is not in the direction that thing is headed!"

"Jack," Paul said firmly, "I hate to say this, but this is my boat. And I say we're gonna follow him. Now just shut up, sit down, and don't interfere." He looked at his distraught friend. "It'll be okay," he said more kindly. "This old boy won't hurt us. He's just showed up to help us. He's going to see us home."

Jack plopped down on one of the damp seat cushions, muttering things about his crazy friend finally going off the deep end. But he sat.

"Now, old feller," Paul said to the giant quietly floating just ahead of the boat. "You're the navigator." He saluted loosely. "I'll follow you."

The great creature's barnacle-spotted body began to move slowly into the fog.

Paul started the engine once again and pushed open the throttle enough to match the whale's speed. He glanced at the compass. The needle was still swinging erratically, useless.

"Guess I have to trust my instincts, and you, old boy," he told the whale. "Let's go."

Together, the whale and the small craft advanced into the thick shroud of fog. Paul thought they must look like a toy following along. He smiled, amused at this image. The whale moved steadily, slowing only to allow Paul to keep him in sight.

Jack said nothing. He peered ahead into the fog, glancing now and again at the whale and shaking his head, tightly gripping the side of the boat.

Paul had no idea how long they had been traveling like this. He had a watch in his pocket, but did not really want to look at it. He thought that, somehow, it would destroy the mood. He simply kept his trust in the whale.

All sense of motion was lost in the fog. The whale's progress was so silent that the sound of the boat motor seemed an intrusion in Paul's mind.

Gradually, Paul became aware of another sound. "Listen, Jack!" he exclaimed. It was the sonorous call of the foghorns ahead of them. The searching, mournful tones, heard at regular intervals, grew louder as they approached.

"*I'll* be damned," Jack breathed. "I never would've believed it."

The whale slowed, allowing the boat to come abreast of its head. Paul cut the engine, and the mist was filled only with the lonesome distant song of the foghorn. The boat drifted gently.

Man and whale observed each other in the silence.

"Thanks, old feller. I appreciate your guiding us in," Paul said softly. "I don't know why you showed up, but I'm mighty pleased you did."

The whale blew a soughing, muted note, its blowhole opening and closing. Then it inhaled deeply, and gently submerged.

Paul and Jack stood together gazing at the now featureless surface of the ocean. Finally Paul turned, a pensive smile creasing his weathered face. He again started the engine. The boat began to move toward the call of the foghorn.

Mary-Alice is happily retired, writing and living by the ocean once more after over half a century working outside the home as an international airline stewardess, expatriate in Japan, professional actor and Las Vegas showgirl, peddler of everything from pencils to public television, police office manager, and miscellaneous other less exotic day jobs. She is a civic activist, wife, mother, grandmother, best friend, and life-long practicing critter lover. The story Mary-Alice relates in "The Guide" happened to her father, Paul, and his friend Jack in June 1954, an experience that her father loved to tell until his death many years later.

Unlikely Bouquet

By Terese Ricci

Fate is the sum total of all of the trivial events that you never thought would amount to anything and that will affect everything forever.

She stares out from the pages of her scrapbook, challenging me to unravel the story of her fate and mine. This album is no longer a mirror into which she peers to find her own youthful reflection. With the passage of time, it has become a fragile window in which I can vaguely see my own blurred image. I did not share in these memories. I struggle to decipher faces, gestures and notes to trace how her life unfolded, seeking to unravel not just a story, but a person. My fate grew from hers, and without the exact sequence of events that the forces of youth, duty, love and geology conspired to arrange, I would not be here today.

Youth

Barbara Nemanich. Her personal record begins near the end of her high school days. She pasted various scraps and mementos into her album: photos, letters, valentines, news clippings and handwritten notes. It is a collage of who she was then. She entitled this section "Funology," the word itself a newsprint cutout.

The only pervasive theme or pattern throughout the album is her presence. On page after page, she smiles out crookedly, trying to conceal an overbite, head tilted slightly downward. Nameless friends swarm around her, clinging like insects on the periphery of her story. In this space, she is the central character.

The Senior Class Presents:
"Green Stockings" by A. E. W. Mason
Friday, April 23, 1924
Produced by special arrangement
with Samuel French of New York
Starring Barbara Nemanich as Madge (Mrs. Rockingham)

Dear Mr. Nemanich:
Your daughter Barbara will graduate next spring. She has done excellent work during her attendance at the Tower-Sudan High School. We are highly pleased with her in every way.

Yours very truly,
BFE, Principal H.S.

CLASS TO FINISH AT TOWER HIGH SCHOOL
Tower, Minn., June 6 (Special to *The Herald*):
Graduation exercises for the Tower-Soudan High School will be held tonight at the school, where Dr. J. W. Holland of St. Paul will give the address. Musical numbers and other features have been arranged.
Miss Hazel Johnson is the salutatorian.
Miss Barbara Nemanich is the valedictorian.

College

Barbara enrolls in college, where perhaps she will continue her study of acting. Brochure pictures of vast dining halls and cloistered dorm rooms decorate the pages. The images are without a single student to disrupt the order of the chairs or scuff the gleaming floors.

A pennant bearing the name Villa St. Scholastica slashes its way across the adjacent page. An unsigned note appears folded over, with simply "I love you, Barbara" scrawled on the torn sheet. She becomes engaged during her first year in college. Maybe he was one of the boys in a football uniform staring stoically outward from a photo taken in front of the school, appearing as naively fearless as a young soldier preparing for war. But this future of continuing in school, of marrying this now nameless boy, was not to be hers.

Duty

The first page of the next section, entitled "Family," bears photographs of all her siblings. Each child has his or her own grouping of pictures trimmed down from larger photos into unlikely and odd shapes. Shards of each childhood hits the eyes like angles of a prism. Some of the photos are somber, Sunday-clothed and posed. Other glimpses are full of smiles and spirit. There are seven children, including herself—names scrawled by each grouping: Barbara, Victoria, George, John, Joseph, Agnes, and Rose. This family is the foundation upon which her identity was built and which almost consumed her entirely.

The next page bears the word "Mother" in iridescent foil lettering. Opposite this page is the picture of a tombstone and a calendar noting the events that happened in swift succession in June and July of 1925.

June 13th: The day I came home for summer vacation from the villa.
June 15th: The day Mother became ill.

June 26th: Mother's last days at home upon this earth. Mother left for Duluth (St. Mary's) at 7:30 a.m., never to return.
July 1st: Mother was operated on.
July 2nd: We all went to Duluth, for Mother was feeling worse.
July 3rd: Mother died at 8:30 am.
July 4th: Mother's body was shipped home.
July 5th: Mother's funeral.

Although in the next pictures, Barbara continues to smile at the camera, the smile is somewhat more tentative. Certain hopes had been dashed. She would not return to school in the fall; she would stay at home to help her father raise the younger children. Instead of continuing as a scholar and an actress, within the course of a few weeks, she assumed the most serious and tragic role in her young life. Barbara at once had lost a mother and become a mother.

Time moved on. She continued to visit her friends at school, although she herself no longer attended. Instead of noting her own achievements, now she tracked the achievements of her friends. Her fiancé broke off the engagement because he would not wait for her indenture to her family to be fulfilled. Her world became smaller. She could only watch as her friends moved on.

During one of these unmarked days, Barbara was courted by another man. He did not appear in the pictures in front of the school. His name was not in the program of a play. He did not ever wear a football uniform. He was one of the boys who had quit school early to become a lumberjack and a miner. Every day he descended deep into the underground mine that was the wellspring of the town. As a barman, his job was to take a heavy bar and chip loose rock from the ceiling of a newly-formed cavern after a dynamite blast. He would be the first person in after the fumes dissipated and the dust settled. He ensured stability and safety for the rest of the crew that followed.

The rock that the mine produced was iron ore, which is enormously dense and strong. The makeup of the rock diminished the typical dangers associated with mining more porous rock, such as coal. Because of its density, the ore was relatively predictable; cave-ins almost never occurred. Silicosis did not plague the lungs. The men emerged with red dust clinging to their clothing and hair instead of black.

As was his nature, Anthony was a silent man, and he made an entrance into her life quietly. He won her affection. He waited for her. When the younger children had grown to adolescence, Barbara looked forward to finally embarking on a married life of her own. She became engaged a second time. Wedding plans were made. Now she would exchange her role as a mother for a role as a wife.

Love

Barbara's sister Rose was only a small girl of perhaps four in the opening pages of the scrapbook. She is the child who stands in front of their mother's knees, tendrils of hair falling down past her shoulders, a half-dozen roses bunched in her small hands, eyes staring blankly into the camera. Shortly before Barbara's wedding, Rose, who by now was eleven years old, was diagnosed with tuberculosis. Later, it would be discovered that Rose had contracted the disease from the school nurse, who for unknown reasons continued to stay in contact with the children at the school despite her illness.

Now I peer through this window into the past and begin filling in the images that are absent on the later pages. I imagine Barbara in the kitchen, involved in some necessary chore, cooking or washing dishes. She is contemplating how she has come to this place in her life twice. Twice on the brink of marriage, and twice sickness and death have joined together to impede her path. As she stares out the kitchen window, a battle is being waged within her as she attempts to balance duty to family and allegiance to herself. When her mother died, she followed the demands of Duty and later lost Love because of it.

It is less than a week before the ceremony is to take place and a decision regarding whether or not to proceed has to be made. Ultimately, she has to make it. Would the dutiful action be to postpone the wedding? Would the selfish action be to proceed? She knows that Anthony will defer to her judgment. Despite the patience he has already exhibited, he will not deliver an ultimatum. However, the simple burden of having to make such a tradeoff is enough to crush her resolve; to cause her to postpone the ceremony to a later, happier day.

There is a knock at the door. Before she has a chance to remove her apron, her parish priest enters.

"Hello, Barbara."

"Hello. Please, sit down," she says, somewhat flustered by his unexpected arrival.

"I've heard the news about Rose. Awful. How is she doing?"

"Her condition is serious. We've sent her to Duluth for confinement."

Barbara has attended mass every Sunday and also attends daily mass during the week. It is a purposeful ritual on her part. She feels validation for her own sacrifice, and the power of the social network embeds her to that purpose. The priest has seen her through the entire saga. He wonders how she is bearing the news. He sits at the kitchen table with her.

"Barbara, I know that you must be considering canceling the wedding."

She looks down at the towel still in her hands. She cannot bear to reveal the turmoil that races within her.

"I am here to encourage you to go through with it, just as planned. I am here to tell you that this is what God would want. God has brought you and Tony together for a reason. And God wants to see you happy."

She nods, her shoulders dropping with relief that a decision has been made.

And here is the wedding picture. Both Barbara and Anthony are posed and somber. She holds an unlikely bouquet of white lilies. A long, flowing gown drapes to the floor. He stares squarely ahead and beyond the camera.

Rose would eventually recover from her illness, but the tradeoff of a life was made that day.

Geology

Although it was an uncommon event, the man who took Anthony's place in the mine during his wedding was killed in an accident. Every night, the enormous chamber that Anthony was assigned to was enlarged by blasting outward and upward until the ceiling came within close proximity to the floor of the mined-out chamber above.

As the wedding photograph was being taken, Anthony's replacement entered the mine chamber after waiting for the dust to settle after a blast. He then proceeded to carefully chip away at the small loose pieces of rock still embedded in the ceiling. What he could not have known was that some of those pieces were precariously holding a massive load of rock in place above his head. The circumstance was created thousands of years earlier when glaciers deposited sediment in this exact, but faulty, stratum. The motion of weather and earth combined to create a less than uniform layer of rock.

The result was that the unfortunate barman was crushed and killed on Barbara and Anthony's wedding day. Had Anthony not been married on that day, he would have been performing the same work in the same chamber and would have been killed in the accident that had been thousands of years in the making.

If Barbara had married her previous fiancé, Anthony would have died. If she simply had stayed in school and continued to pursue drama, he would have died. If she had not agreed to marry him, he would have died. Perhaps she might have cut the news from the paper and pasted it into her album, a sad memorial to a boy from her hometown.

For me, this is the story about how my grandparents came together. I have been told that I have inherited Barbara's eyes and the bridge of her nose. In my own memory of her, I can only envision the tint of her hair, the shape of her eyeglasses, the spots on her hands, the vague smell of powder that always engulfed her.

She died when I was five. But all I really have to do is look into the mirror to see her staring back. Part of her has been preserved in me. Some small evidence of immortality. She always said that she saved her husband's life by marrying him. In this way, she will remain at the center of my story forever.

Terese Ricci lives in Northern California with her husband and two beloved dachshunds. She has an MBA from the University of Minnesota and an MFA in Creative Writing from the University of San Francisco. She is currently working on her first novel.

THE MYSTERY OF FATE:

What Is Fate?

I believe that almost all significant things are controlled by fate. What family we are born into. What genes we are born with. Whether we are black, white, red or yellow. What preferences we have. If we cross the street at four o'clock and find a winning lottery ticket lying in the gutter. If we cross that same street an hour later and get hit by a car. Some things we can control, mainly attitude, resolve and our power to reason. Other than those, and some of the positives or negatives stemming from them, I say it's all up to fate. Or maybe what I'm really saying is it's all up to whoever created this world and controls it.

Jerry Bower
Writer, retired farmer, adventurer

THE MYSTERY OF FATE:

A Mother's Heart Always Knows

By Lisa Ricard Claro

In 1965, I was five years old. In those days, riding in the car meant standing with my tippy-toes on the floor of the front passenger side, hanging onto and peering over the dash as I watched the world fly past the windshield. The statistics that frightened future parents into securing their children with restraints were unknown at that time. Looking back, it is a wonder so many of us survived the dangers of the road.

On this particular day, there were two things which occurred that cemented my belief in a higher power. One was a decision made by my mother, and the other was an uncanny perception by my grandmother.

My older brother and sister required my mother to play the role of taxi driver. They had a birthday party to attend. It was a Saturday afternoon in a parade of similar Saturday afternoons, with nothing to mark it as anything more or less than normal. I can still see my mother holding her purse and her keys, and my brother and sister heading out to the carport. It was bad enough that they were going to a party and I was not; I did not understand why my mother was refusing my desire to ride along. I pleaded and begged and even resorted to whining, but to no avail. My mother remained steadfast in her refusal to take me with them.

"Why can't she go?" my father asked. "What's the big deal?"

"I really don't know why," Mama said after a moment's hesitation. "I just know she can't come."

And that was that. The door closed, and I stood at the front window watching through a blur of tears as the car pulled out of the driveway and disappeared around the corner. My grandmother, who lived with us, came over and gave me a big hug.

"C'mon," she said. "Let's go color."

"I don't want to color," I whimpered. "I want to be with my mommy!" And so saying, I remained at the window, intent on staying put until my mother's car pulled back into the driveway.

Grandma, always one to offer comfort, went to her room to collect her sewing and returned to the living room to keep me company during my vigil.

My child's memory offers no reference of how long a time it was between my mother's departure and the sudden blaring of sirens in the distance. This I do recall with full clarity: standing at the window, a sad sentinel, and turning away only when I heard my grandmother gasp for no apparent reason from her seat on the couch behind me.

"Frank!" she cried out for my father. "Frank!"

"What is it?" Daddy rushed into the room.

"The sirens!" Grandma's eyes were wide and frightened. "The sirens! They're for our Millie."

After dropping off my sister and brother at the party, my mother's car was struck broadside while pulling through an intersection. The car was hit with enough force to spin it around and knock my mother unconscious. Suffering internal injuries,

Mama was rushed to the hospital for emergency surgery. By the grace of God, she fully recovered and came home to us.

The passenger side of the vehicle, the place where I would have been sitting had I been with her, was demolished. If I had accompanied my mother on that routine Saturday drive, I probably would have been killed.

When asked later what instinct had compelled her to deny my request to ride along, Mama could only shake her head and say, "I don't know. I just knew I couldn't take her with me."

I once asked Grandma how she knew the sirens were for my mother. Grandma said that when Mama remained resolute in her decision to leave me behind, with no ostensible motive, she believed there was a reason. When she heard the sirens, her heart knew what that reason was.

"A mother's heart always knows," said Grandma.

Lisa Ricard Claro's publishing credits include stories in the anthology books *Chicken Soup for the Beach Lover's Soul* and *Cup of Comfort for Dog Lovers.* Lisa lives with her family in Georgia, where she is a frequent contributor of personal essays and humor columns to the *Atlanta Journal-Constitution.*

Fate on the Fly

By Brenda Warneka

It is in your moments of decision that your destiny is shaped.

Anthony Robbins

The engraved invitation rests in a silver frame on my husband Dick's desk. The ink is fading after years of the Arizona sun beating on it through his office window. It reads:

The family of Mr. and Mrs. Donald E. Day
Request the pleasure of your company
At a buffet dinner to celebrate
The fiftieth anniversary of their marriage
On Sunday, the sixteenth of August, at four o'clock
At Westcourt in the Buttes
2000 Westcourt Way, Tempe, Arizona

The invitation arrived in the mail near the end of July 1987. Donald and Genevieve Day were the parents of our friends, brothers Don and Bill Day, and we were pleased that they were including us in their anniversary celebration. This was a party we did not want to miss. The problem was that Dick, the president of our family-owned company, planned to spend the week before the Days' party working in our Detroit office, and his parents were expecting him to stay on to visit them in Erie, Pennsylvania, over that weekend. Dick almost always visited his parents when he went to Detroit on business because his father was eighty-eight years old, his mother eighty, and he knew each visit with them could be the last.

Family members and friends were familiar with Dick's routine of winding up business trips to Detroit with a weekend visit to his parents' home in Erie, which was less than an hour away from Detroit by commuter airline. He would then normally take a late Sunday afternoon commuter flight from Erie back to Detroit in time to catch Northwest Airlines Flight 255, which left Detroit at 8:45 p.m. to fly non-stop to Phoenix.

This schedule allowed Dick to spend the most time with his parents, and with the time change, still get back to Phoenix at a reasonable hour. He always traveled by Northwest Airlines to get the mileage to qualify for its annual "Gold Card."

If Dick kept to his normal schedule, however, and returned to Phoenix on Northwest Airlines Flight 255 on the day of the Days' anniversary, he would miss the party, so he changed his reservations. He arranged to leave Erie on a morning commuter flight to Detroit, about five hours earlier than usual, and then catch an earlier Northwest flight from Detroit back to Phoenix.

Dick remembers his father saying to him when he dropped him off at the Erie Airport, "I wish you would stay longer, Richard," and his response, "I would, Dad, but we have this party in Arizona tonight."

Upon Dick's arrival home, I picked him up at Phoenix's Sky Harbor Airport, drove directly to Westcourt in the Buttes, a beautiful resort, and we had a wonderful time partying with the Day family and friends until late into the evening.

When we stepped into the kitchen upon our arrival home, the flashing light on the telephone answering machine caught our attention. To our bewilderment, the machine was loaded with frantic messages from family members and friends begging to know if Dick was safe and imploring us to return their calls when we got home, regardless of the hour.

With our first returned call to our son Jim, we learned that Northwest Airlines Flight 255 had gone out of control during takeoff from the Wayne County Airport, smashed into a highway overpass, and exploded. We had not had occasion to tell most of our family members and friends that Dick was taking an earlier flight back to Phoenix that Sunday, and they assumed that, as usual, he was on Flight 255. Upon hearing a breaking news story on television that the plane had crashed, Jim was so sure his stepfather was onboard, he had fallen to his knees and started to pray for him.

Described in later court proceedings as the "second-worst aviation disaster in American history," the crash killed 154 passengers and crew members (everyone onboard except one four-year-old girl) and two people on the ground. Investigators concluded that the crash occurred because the pilot forgot to set the wing flaps before takeoff.

If not for the Days having chosen August 16 as their wedding date and inviting us to their party half a century later, Dick would have been in the wrong place at the wrong time—aboard Northwest Flight 255—and I would have been a widow. It is as though Dick was supposed to die, and by pure chance (or *was it?*), something that happened fifty years earlier gave him a reason to change his plans, and saved his life.

Although the ink on the party invitation is fading with the passage of time, the emotional impact on me when I read it today is as powerful as it was when I looked at it, in awe, the day after the party.

Could This Be Fate?

By Jeannette Gardner

Twenty years ago I used to go to the Club Palomino in Toronto, where I loved listening to good bands and dancing to country music. I frequently dragged my girlfriend along to see my favorite band, Cheyenne. The group always packed the place, and my friend and I loved to get up and dance to what we thought was amazing music. I was particularly interested in the rhythm guitar player. To me, he was the best-looking member of the band, and I loved his voice, along with his unique rhythm guitar sound. Yes, I was attracted to him, and I goggle-eyed him playing his guitar while I was dancing to the music or sitting at a table listening. I've always had this thing for bands. I play guitar myself and have dreams of playing in a band.

Cheyenne was the most popular band at the Club Palomino, and I went there every chance I got to hear it perform, and, of course, I always had my eyes on my favorite player. I often saw him during breaks with a blonde woman and assumed she was his girlfriend or wife.

As the saying goes, all good things come to an end, and to my great dismay, the Club Palomino closed—for good. A huge townhouse subdivision was built in its place. So all the bands were gone, including my favorite. When I first found out about the club closing, I wanted to approach Cheyenne, particularly the rhythm guitar player, and ask where the band would play in the future, but I did not have the nerve.

15 YEARS LATER

As time went on, I met someone and got married. That was a mistake! Eventually, we got divorced, and I started going with friends to dance clubs again, but I tired of it after not meeting anyone of interest, and pretty much stopped going.

One day, a friend suggested I join a particular dating website on the Internet, which I *never* thought I would do. I decided to check it out for fun, as I had heard so much about it from people who even said they had met their "soul mates" from that particular site, and were now happily married. Surprisingly, I had a few dates with men from the site, meeting in public places, but I just did not find the right person, and I thought I never would through a dating website. I sort of gave up on it, until one night ...

After getting home from a dance club, I sat down at my computer. When I logged onto that same dating website again, there was an interesting e-mail from a man named Rick, whose picture I liked. He wrote that he liked my picture and profile. The words "music" and "guitar" in my profile had caught his eye. We started emailing each other and discovered that we had a lot in common, especially our mutual interest in music. Also, he was Bulgarian, and I was Hungarian—in East European culture, a desirable match, as our ancestors had a common origin. How usual was that between two Canadians? Our families lived in the same small town, north of Toronto: Richmond Hill, of all places, and we had even been born in the same hospital in Toronto, though in different years. After that, we "chatted" every night as often as we could.

Once we got onto the subject of music, we found out that we both liked country music, and we both wrote songs. I told

Rick that I had frequented a particular club several years before, which had closed. Of course, he asked me the name of the club, and I told him the Club Palomino. He expressed surprise, and said he used to play there. I wasn't sure whether or not to believe him. He said he would send me a picture by e-mail attachment of his band that played there. I thought *Oh sure!* as I waited patiently in front of my computer for the picture to arrive.

Lo and behold, a huge picture appeared on my computer screen with a caption announcing CHEYENNE - CLUB PALOMINO. It was a photo of the Cheyenne band from fifteen years before, and there was a young man playing the rhythm guitar—my favorite player whom I had thought was so cute!

I was absolutely stunned. It was unbelievable! Like a miracle had suddenly happened. Like a fairy tale! Rick and I continued emailing back and forth for several weeks, and eventually we exchanged phone numbers. We then started talking on the phone every night. All the things we had in common were amazing! It was just too good to be true.

Rick remembered having met my friend whom I was with at the Club Palomino years before, and he also remembered having seen us dancing to the music of his band. I know his eyes and mine had to have met at some point during that time. It was a very strange feeling having crossed paths some fifteen years earlier ... and now, talking together in the present, and remembering. The blonde girl he had been with at the Club Palomino was the girl he eventually married for eight years before they, too, were divorced.

After about three weeks of talking on the phone, chatting on the Internet and exchanging more pictures, we decided to meet at the Canadian Legion Hall for a cup of coffee and to become better acquainted.

The Canadian Legion Hall has an open "stage night," when people can go up on stage and perform. Rick had played there before, so he asked me if I minded if he went up on the stage to do a solo. He did not need to ask. A good-looking man whom I'd had a crush on so many years ago strumming his guitar and singing to me would be heaven.

He got up on the stage and started playing his guitar and singing in front of an audience, but I felt like he was singing just for me—just *to* me. I was hooked!

Evidently, Rick was hooked, too, because now, five years later, we are still together, playing music and laughing about how we "re-met on the Net." The final surprise was the first time we looked out the window of our new condo, and to our astonishment, what did we see? We saw the office building of the dating website where we had met, of all things. What a coincidence that was!

What if I had not decided to give that certain dating website one more chance? I just know it was an angel on my shoulder who guided me to do exactly that, and to finally find happiness and true love. It is funny how life is ... it seems our marriage was not meant to be years before, but fate finally brought us together at the right time and place.

Jeannette Gardner lives in Etobicoke, Canada, where she works as a medical secretary at a private clinic. Fascinated by music and popular bands (she saw the Beatles live three times), she taught herself to play guitar and began writing songs. Her hope is that a major artist will record one of her songs. This story is dedicated to her mother, Elizabeth, who passed away in May 2007, battling cancer at the age of eighty, and who had encouraged Jeannette to write the story. The title "Could This Be Fate?" is a song Jeannette wrote for Rick Ivanoff, which you can hear on her website: www.tenderangelmusic.com.

God Writes Straight Lines
In Crooked Letters

By Arlene Uslander

My mother used the expression "God writes straight lines in crooked letters" often when I was a child, only I never knew what it meant. I think I do now.

It all started with a rock—an ordinary, flat rock. My husband and I, both Chicagoans, were in Arizona visiting our friends Brenda and Dick Warneka. Little did I realize that God was going to lead me along a path (literally) that eventually would save, or at the very least, prolong, my life.

I had promised my eleven-year-old grandson, Ryan, that while I was in Arizona, I would find a white rock, write his name on it with a marker, and hide it somewhere outside the Warnekas' house. Ryan and his parents were going to Arizona for Ryan's spring break shortly after my husband and I were due home, and the plan was for him to try to find the rock. If he did, I would give him a prize.

One morning, my husband and I walked through a construction site where there were many flat, white rocks. I sifted through the dirt until I found just the right one. When we got back to my friends' house, I wrote Ryan's name on it and put it on the front porch in a potted plant.

Several days later when we flew back to Chicago, I started to feel sick, and during the four-hour flight, I slept the whole time. Once we got home I began to cough, and I broke out in a terrible itching rash that covered my whole body.

The following morning I went to see my internist. After listening to my lungs, he ordered a chest X-ray. The X-ray showed that I had pneumonia, but it also showed some strange looking "bumps and nodules" on my lungs. After a lung scan, my internist, who was noticeably alarmed, sent me to a pulmonologist. My husband accompanied me to the pulmonologist's office. The doctor minced no words. He said there was a strong possibility that I had metastatic lung cancer. He wanted me to make an appointment with a thoracic surgeon right away.

In a state of complete shock, my husband and I were almost out the door when the doctor called out," Oh, by the way, where were you on your vacation?" We had told him sometime during the visit that we had just come back from a trip. When we told him Arizona, he said matter-of-factly, "You know, they have some strange diseases out there—especially one called Valley Fever." That was all he said, and we left.

As soon as I got home, I e-mailed Brenda and told her what was going on. She did an Internet search and wrote me back, saying that, according to my symptoms, she thought I did have Valley Fever. My husband and I were very excited after reading the information she faxed us. Valley Fever (the scientific name is *Cocidioidis Immitis)* is a treatable disease, indigenous to the Southwest, caused by a fungus that affects the lungs. People contract it from spores in the air, or the ground, especially in construction areas where the dirt has been disturbed, which was exactly where I had been digging!

My husband and I went to see the internist again. Like many doctors in the Midwest, he had never treated anyone with Valley Fever, but he agreed that the symptoms certainly seemed to match mine. He scheduled a blood test for me that same day, and informed us that it would take about two weeks to get the results.

What a long two weeks (and a lot of prayers) that was! But, two weeks to the day, which happened to be my birthday, the doctor called and excitedly told me that I did indeed have Valley Fever, and he wanted me to see an infectious disease doctor. It didn't appear to be cancer after all. What a wonderful, wonderful birthday present!

The following week, an infectious disease specialist put me on anti-fungal medication for Valley Fever. He told me to have another lung scan in six months, which I did. In the meantime, I had no symptoms at all. I felt great!

There was good news and bad news. The good news was, the follow-up lung scan showed that my lungs looked much better. The bad news was that I still had one nodule on my left lung. The internist wanted me to have a P.E.T. scan, which identifies suspicious areas in the body by lighting up tumors. Four days later, I got the results. The nodule lit up. Next came a biopsy. Positive: lung cancer!

The whole thing seemed like a crazy dream. Here I had been diagnosed with Valley Fever, with absolutely no symptoms of lung cancer, but all of a sudden I *did* have cancer.

The following week, I had surgery to remove the nodule. I subsequently underwent chemotherapy and radiation.

At the time of the present writing, it is four years since my surgery. I am feeling fine, but must have a lung scan every three months. So I have to say thank heavens for Valley Fever! I am also thankful that my friend invited me to Arizona, where I contracted it. And last but certainly not least, I am grateful to my grandson Ryan, because if not for him and his upcoming trip to

Arizona, I would not have been digging in the dirt looking for a rock (not one of my customary habits!), and it is probably there and then that I picked up Valley Fever.

What if I had not contracted an infection for which I needed a follow up lung scan? And if I hadn't had to have that second scan, who knows when or if that malignant nodule would have been discovered?

As my mother used to say, "Sometimes God writes straight lines in crooked letters." I understand now that my mother meant that sometimes God presents a simple message in an obscure way.

Writing my grandson's name on a rock was the obscure way for me.

Tara's Journey

By Patricia Hopper Patteson

Fate is a power beyond my control that determines what happens. Can I change it? Yes and no. By studying the consequences of the situation, I can sometimes soften the results.

Garnet Hunt White

I wonder about one of life's great mysteries: why an inevitable safety net catches some young people and lets others fall through.

My daughter, Tara, began using marijuana when she was about fifteen. Her personality changed from kind, loving and considerate to distrustful and belligerent. She stopped being an excellent student who was active in gymnastics, basketball, and martial arts, and started hanging out with friends at late night parties. I thought this was typical teenage rebellion at first. Then I discovered a marijuana pipe that she had carelessly left lying around her bedroom.

When I confronted her, she denied any drug use and said that the pipe belonged to a friend. For over a year, her behavior continued to deteriorate, and there were many outbursts between us. I even arranged a meeting with a family therapist, hoping to find some solutions that would make our home life more tolerable, but the counselor couldn't get Tara to admit that she was a marijuana user.

Tara's habit escalated to the point that she skipped school, drove with other students to remote locations, and spent her days getting high. Desperate to resolve the situation, I finally decided to have her tested for drugs. The day before her appointment, Tara packed up her belongings and moved out of the house. She went to live with her father from whom I had been divorced for many years. Even though my ex-husband lived in the same town, we had no communication, and he had no idea what was happening with Tara. I knew he would refuse to speak to me on the phone or in person, so I wrote him a letter.

It was useless; he did not believe me. However, it wasn't long before he discovered for himself that Tara had a problem. Things between them soon escalated out of control, so much so that he didn't object when she drifted toward living with her best friend, Jennifer. Jennifer's mother gave the girls the freedom they wanted.

Jennifer's family lived near my home. When I learned that Tara had taken up residence there, I immediately filed a referral for a runaway with the Sheriff's Office. After I told Tara what I had done, she moved back to her father's house. Things between them did not improve, so she called and asked to come back home.

A month later, Tara and I attended a hearing in Juvenile Court, presided over by Judge Mullins, who, in a very calm and direct manner, told Tara the consequences if she continued down her chosen path. He pointed out there was evidence that she was using marijuana, and combined with falling grades, this did not bode well for her.

The judge told Tara that because she refused to listen to her parents, she had to answer to society. Her curfew was set for 8:00 p.m. on week nights and 11:00 p.m. on weekends. She was to check in with the Probation Office at appointed times and be tested periodically for drugs. In addition, she had to attend weekly drug and alcohol abuse meetings. She was to go to school every day and attend all classes. If she strayed from these conditions, there would be another hearing, the rules would become more stringent, and she could be sent to a juvenile home. In such places, the judge said, there would be no freedom. She would be told when to get up, when to eat, when to watch TV, and when she could make a phone call. In essence, her freedom would be taken away.

I will always be grateful to Judge Mullins for attempting to make my daughter realize the seriousness of the situation. Tara and I both left the small courtroom in tears.

The judge did not realize it, but by restricting Tara's activities, he may have saved her life. Less than a week after the hearing, Jennifer made plans to visit relatives living about two hundred miles away. Jennifer's cousin, Denise, who had been visiting from out of town and was returning home, pleaded with Jennifer and Tara to go back with her for a few days. Jennifer had already made up her mind to go, and told Tara they would have a great time partying with Denise.

But it was too soon. Tara had not had a chance to prove she could behave herself, and she knew she would never receive permission to go; not from the judge or me. Downhearted, she said goodbye to her friends.

The next day, Jennifer and Denise left, but they never made it to Denise's house. They were close to the end of their trip when Jennifer asked Denise to let her drive. They had been drinking throughout the journey, and even though Jennifer had very little experience behind the wheel, she wanted to drive. Denise was easily convinced. Soon afterward, Jennifer misjudged a curve in the road and lost control of the car. She was thrown through the windshield because she didn't have her seatbelt on and was killed instantly. Denise, who had been wearing her seatbelt, suffered a broken arm.

Tara did not get the news directly; it came to her by way of a friend. She called me at work, hysterical. It was impossible for her to believe that Jennifer was dead. Hadn't she just spoken to her the previous day? *How could it be?* The shock of losing her friend under such tragic circumstances was very difficult for Tara's teenage mind to comprehend. Death did not come to healthy, young girls.

Several days later, Jennifer's body was brought back home so that family and friends could say goodbye. Her cousin Denise, with her arm in a cast and sling, was a stark reminder of the accident that had ended her cousin's short life.

Jennifer had chosen to be an organ donor and had been on life support after the accident so that her vital organs could be used to save other lives. Her mother had acquiesced to her decision. I was amazed that someone so young would think ahead to make such a choice.

At Jennifer's memorial service, Tara and others spoke about what Jennifer meant to them. Tara wrote a long poem, but the part that touched me most was when she said, "They say that hearts don't really break, but that's not true. For today, when Jennifer is laid to rest, it breaks our hearts in two."

Tara has a written reminder of her friend that she keeps in her scrapbook. In a poem entitled "The Trizick and the Snow Cricket," Jennifer wrote: "The trizick and the snow cricket will rule forever, because the friendship we have will never die. She will always be in my heart, for the trizick and snow cricket will never part."

Jennifer had loved dolphins and the ocean. A few days after the memorial service, her mother took her ashes to the sea to spread on the waves. She invited Tara along, but Tara was already back in school and couldn't take a week off, which is how long Jennifer's mother was gone. On the morning that Jennifer's mother spread the ashes, dolphins appeared and played very close to shore.

Many things plague my mind about Jennifer's death. Mostly, I think about the circumstances that prevented Tara from being with her best friend on that fatal trip. For someone as young as Jennifer to have become an organ donor is enough to make me question whether she had a subconscious premonition that her life would be short-lived.

Jennifer's death had a profound effect on Tara and her friends. They all had had their drivers' licenses for some time, but before Jennifer's death, they rarely strapped on their seatbelts, even when under the influence of alcohol or drugs. And most of them had already been involved in minor fender-benders. Since Jennifer's death, the drug use has stopped, they no longer drink and drive, and they make it a point to always fasten their seatbelts. Perhaps Jennifer's death has saved other lives.

One thing is sure: Jennifer's tragic death will never be forgotten by Tara, who could just as easily have accompanied her down that ill-fated road.

It is now eleven years later. Tara has earned a B.A. in Environmental Geoscience from West Virginia University. She is professionally employed at a local firm and is working on her Master's degree in Environmental Microbiology.

Patricia Hopper Patteson is a native of Dublin, Ireland, who lives in West Virginia. She earned an M.A. and B.A. from West Virginia University. Her fiction and non-fiction have appeared in magazines and anthologies. She is currently completing her novels *Kilpara* and *Lough Corrib.* Patricia credits her writing ability to her storytelling parents, who made every family outing an experience in detail and imagination.

Closure

By Barbara Yavitt

In 1973, my husband, our three teenagers and I excitedly traveled to Europe, the children having saved for the excursion by doing odd jobs and sacrificing birthday and holiday gifts. Our kids were nationally-ranked swimmers in the U.S. who kept in shape while we were away by training with government-sponsored swimming teams in the countries we visited: England, France, Holland, and Belgium. The trip was a very special and informative one. We went to museums, parks, zoos, galleries and many historical sites, as well as wonderful ethnic restaurants and theaters. Everywhere we went, we met interesting people.

We undertook a more somber activity in Belgium when we decided to visit Breendonk, one of the smaller Nazi concentration camps in Europe during World War II. Breendonk is located about twelve miles from Antwerp in what was one of a chain of fortresses originally built prior to World War I to defend Belgium against a German attack. The day we arrived was rainy and overcast, and soon our moods matched the weather.

As we toured, we learned about the horrors that took place at the camp, which included segregation of prisoners according to how the Nazis ranked their desirability and determined such things as space between sleeping cots, bathroom privileges allowed, and the number of meals provided in a day. The better accommodations went to Belgium common criminals, followed by those the Nazis considered deviants; then political prisoners, followed by enemy soldiers captured by the Nazis; and finally, the very worst living conditions were for Jewish inmates who were in transit to death camps such as Auschwitz. Jews were not given blankets, were forced to wear armbands marked with the Star of David, and were at times shackled in leg irons.

We viewed rooms used for torture and interrogation of the prisoners. Execution by shooting or hanging was said to be common, although Breendonk was not a place with gas chambers.

At the end of the tour, we went up some stairs to a large room where there were glass cases filled with items that had been worn by or were taken from the prisoners. The Nazis, being very methodical, had left books of records concerning each and every inmate imprisoned at this facility. On the top shelf of one of the glass counters was an open record book, and I saw that the very first name listed on the page was that of an American soldier: Martin Pearson. He had died of dysentery very early in his confinement.

The experience at Breendonk left all of us with haunting memories that we will never forget.

A few days later, we flew back to the States, our suitcases loaded with gifts, pictures and souvenirs. Each of us had many people whom we looked forward to telling about our experiences. About a week after we had settled back into our normal daily routines, I took pictures, books, maps and a few gifts to Alice Monson, our lovely neighbor across the street who had moved to Arizona from North Dakota.

First, I gave Alice the gifts that I had brought back for her; then I started to talk nonstop about all the things we had done and seen on our trip to Europe. When I got to the part about Breendonk, I brought out brochures and a small book that was written in French about the concentration camp. I told Alice the horrific details, including the record book with the entry about the captured American soldier who had died of dysentery. When I mentioned his rank, name and age, Alice's face turned pale, and she started to sob. Pearson was her maiden name, and the young soldier, Martin, was her brother, reported missing in action. Alice's family had never known what had happened to him, and if he had died, how he had died.

We hugged each other.

Barbara Yavitt is a Chicago native and has a B.S. in Education from Northwestern University. She taught elementary grades in the Chicago public schools prior to moving with her husband, Richard, and their children to Scottsdale, Arizona, in 1969. She has a son, twin daughters, and four grandchildren. Since 1994, she has been a facilitator for literacy, chairing a monthly book discussion group open to the public, which is sponsored by the City of Scottsdale and the Scottsdale Public Library. Her hobbies include travel, writing poetry, and multimedia painting and sculpture.

Better Lucky Than Good

By Dave Gitomer

Fate is the ultimate trickster. It often has the king when the queen is played and then for a lark, it plays the three when you have the four. Often skill is not the determinant of the outcome; it is just dumb luck. Yes, and the brilliance is often coincidence—or is it?

As I boarded the Long Island Railroad commuter train on my way to work at the New York Stock Exchange, I was thinking that stock trading, in spite of recent technological changes, is still nothing but a game of chance. There are millions to be made, and millions to be lost. My father was a trader who owned a seat on the exchange. He wasn't the best at his job or the worst, but he did manage to raise a family comfortably.

Taking my seat next to the window, I reflected on how the stock market's recent volatility was causing so much pain to the average investor. When it's on its way up, people love it too much, and when it's going down, they shut their eyes. The crazed emotions that greed creates make the business. The new computer-driven agents amplify the gyrations. At times I would be on top of the situation and on the right side, and then, as fast as a microprocessor could spit out orders, I was "under the ice." This new way of doing things was disconcerting. I often wondered what my old man would make of it.

As the train rolled onward, the New York City skyline came into view. My stomach tightened; I was nearing the battleground. My pulse raced as the spires of commerce neared. I would soon have to decide how to play the market. Should I be a buyer or a seller? I always thumbed through my printout of current positions at this point. Today it seemed that I might be a bit on the long side. This could be dangerous. I glanced at the newspaper of the fellow sitting next to me. The headline screamed "New Financial Millennia Coming." There were also articles about a White House sex scandal and North Korea testing missiles.

"Well," I mused, "if it's in the *New York Times,* everyone knows it already." Luckily, my wife was now working, and, if I screwed up, we could still last awhile. I was wondering how much longer I could continue in this business. The stress was killing me. The hours were short—we started at 9:30 a.m. and got out at 4:00 p.m.—but the time in-between seemed eternal. I needed a way out. I had to make the big hit: the last big score that would allow me to clip coupons from treasury bonds for the rest of my life.

I ran the plan through my mind. It would be the final battle—I would margin to the hilt and shoot it all. An all-or-nothing stratagem began to formulate in my mind as the train pulled into Penn Station. My thoughts were distracted by the masses of commuters rushing from the train to catch the subway. It was chaos. Briefcases and umbrellas were flying.

This was not a time to formulate a detailed strategy. I picked up my laptop and scurried off the train. I was in a hurry along with everyone else. Suddenly, I felt a push from behind. I looked down and saw a coin, then stooped to pick it up. It was a silver dollar. I laughed and put it in my pocket. Then, as I came up to the newsstand, I turned to the vendor.

"One Quick Pick lottery ticket, please. I just found this dollar; this could be my lucky day." I was laughing as I finished the sentence. The vendor gave me the ticket without so much as a nod. I folded it, put it in my pocket, and hurried onto the subway train.

I was sweating; my heart was beating faster and faster. Wall Street grew closer and closer. It was not a heart attack, but the rising tension was not subsiding either. I clutched my laptop for dear life. Wall Street was the next stop.

I exited the subway. As I walked, I looked into other traders' faces for signs. The emotions were mixed. I was almost frozen in fear. As I neared the exchange, I wanted out. The neon sign of a nearby bar caught my eye. It was calling me big time, but I would not allow myself to go in this early in the day. I lit a smoke to relax. I leaned against an old building to steady myself.

Suddenly, as if by magic, I came up with a plan. I was going to go long on IBM shares. Yes, that was it. Shoot for the moon; the trade was now coming. I would buy it on the opening bell, and if those computers went my way, I would be out of there at four o'clock and in the chips. Filled with self-confidence, I finished my cigarette and entered the exchange building.

Big John from Merrill Lynch filled the order and looked at me as though he thought I was crazy. Maybe I was, but I felt I would be the one laughing on settlement day. Then an announcement crossed the tape, "Greenspan resigns." The buzz was incredible and the market tanked. Not dropped, but *tanked*. The flood of sell orders from the computers was relentless. The stocks were dropping like rockets.

"Oh, hell!" I muttered. I was caught on the wrong side of the trade. Then I decided to execute the second leg of the trade. "Selling ten thousand IBMs at market!" I screamed desperately into the crowd.

"Be careful, guy. This is a fast market." Big John shook his head as he filled the order. Now I was cash-strapped. I had to liquidate more long positions. Rapidly, I began to go from post to post, selling myself out to cover my margin commitment. The market was falling faster and faster. My head was spinning. Then another buzz passed on the broad tape: "Correction: Greenspan not resigning." The computers reversed positions and drove the market higher.

I was wiped out. My instincts had betrayed me. Realizing the damage was done, I called it a day and walked across the street into the bar.

"Double vodka and beer chaser," I bellowed.

"Hey, it's only 10 a.m. You sure?" asked the bartender. He had seen this look before. He got the drinks.

"Bad day, huh?" he inquired as he set the glasses on the counter. "Well, stuff happens; maybe tomorrow will be better."

"Yeah," I murmured, carrying my drink over to a table. I wasn't in the mood to talk to anyone.

After a few rounds, things got hazy. I left the bar and went to the subway. I don't remember much of the trip home. When I got there, I went to bed. I had missed supper with the family. On bad trading days, they knew better than to bother me. I woke up in the middle of the night and made my way to the computer to see the damages.

My brokerage accounts came up on the computer screen; the balances were severely drawn down. Major trouble! I sat on the couch and began to cry. I went for my suit jacket, rummaging through the pockets for cigarettes. Suddenly, I found the Lotto ticket. I laughed hysterically, went back to the computer again, logged onto the Lotto website, and began to check the numbers.

Pencil in hand, I started circling the numbers. Four, yes, I had that; 6, yes, I had that; 18, yes, I had that. I began to perspire. Then 26, yes, I had that. I had won at least the four-number pool. But fate was not stopping there. I needed a 32, and yes, I had it. I was in the five-number pool. Then I screamed with joy—53. I hit the big one! Yes, the silver dollar I had found had bought the winning Lotto ticket.

My screams woke the whole house. My two daughters and wife rushed into the living room. I began to relate the tale, telling them how I had gotten whipsawed and had blown everything. Well, almost everything. Then I showed them the lottery ticket that had just made us rich. We all hugged and smiled at the Grace of the Fates.

Dave Gitomer is a New York poet who writes and has done performance poetry on Internet, radio, and at cafes. He showcases his work on America Online and has been featured on *Poetic Spotlight.* He likes to read books on philosophy, especially those with an Eastern slant. Although written in first person, Dave points out that the story, "Better Lucky than Good," happened to a good friend of his. Does Dave buy lottery tickets? You will just have to ask him.

I Am a Man ~ You Are a Woman

By Xujun Eberlein

Growing up in the isolated People's Republic of China, I had never in my wildest imagination thought an American would walk into my life. By 1987, however, the "reform and opening-up" era started by China's then-leader Deng Xiaoping had unfolded in its full glory. After being closed to the outside world for almost four decades, China's door was finally open, and open wide. Not only did private businesses prosper as might bamboo shoots after a spring rain, but foreigners also gushed in looking for everything from a lacquered rice bowl to an exotic experience.

Bob, an American scientist with a Ph.D. in Management from MIT and a "bicyclist at large" (as he referred to himself), had come to Shanghai to teach a graduate class in Economics and chair an international conference. The international conference would take several months of preparation with the host university. He brought along his Trek touring bike, planning an ambitious ride to Tibet—a place that held great mystery for him—after the conference was over.

While Bob was in Shanghai, a Chinese professor and friend, Wang, mentioned to him that he had been invited to give a speech at the Chengdu University of Science and Technology, or CUST. Bob looked at the map and saw that Chengdu was at the edge of Tibet, near the ultimate destination of his planned bike trip. Intrigued, he enthusiastically volunteered to go with Professor Wang, and give his own presentation.

This was where random process, mother of mankind, came into play: At the time of Bob's visit, I was a graduate student at the Chengdu Branch of the Chinese Academy of Sciences, studying Systems Science in the Applied Mathematics Institute. Though my institute was only a few minutes' bike ride from CUST, except for that fateful April day in 1987, I had never attended a single lecture there.

It should be explained that at the time, among mainland Chinese people, any balanced attitude toward foreigners, especially Americans, was rare, and I was not an exception. The veneration of white foreigners as being superior was as common as the revulsion for their perceived vile actions, the roots of both attitudes being traced as far back as the Opium Wars in the mid-nineteenth century. I was in the latter camp, a heritage passed on from my parents whose hatred toward America had developed in the 1940s.

Li, a student of Professor Wang's, whom I had recently met at a conference, was scheduled to serve as the translator for the American professor's lecture at neighboring CUST. Li came to my dorm the day before and urged me to attend. "See how good my translation is," he exclaimed. With my recalcitrant attitude, it was only reluctantly that I agreed to go hear the American scholar talk on System Dynamics, a subject I was studying.

I went to the lecture with two classmates, Zhang and Zhou, and sat in the back of the large auditorium. Imagine my astonishment when at the end of his presentation, the lecturer jumped down from the stage, joined the dissipating crowd walking toward the back of the auditorium, and came up to me speaking English!

I must say that during Bob's lecture, though I hardly followed the cadence of his foreign language (my English was poor then), his discussion of System Dynamics and his academic manner cast quite a different image from that of other foreigners who were flocking to China at the time to take easy English-teaching jobs. There was intelligence in his shy demeanor that I seldom saw in men this young, native or foreign. I certainly did not expect a stranger, let alone a foreign stranger, to single out my average face from a large audience.

"*Nihao.*" the American stood right before me, greeting me in toneless Chinese, then switched to English. "Are you a student here?"

I understood this simple question but could not find the right word to answer it.

"No," my two classmates, eager to converse in English, answered for me.

"Where do you study?" Bob asked me, with deliberately slow enunciation.

Again, I understood the question, but could not form an English response. I opened and closed my mouth a few times, feeling my face getting hot with embarrassment, no words coming out. Zhang and Zhou jumped at the opportunity to engage in a stuttered English conversation with the American, whose eyes were on me while he answered them. I finally burst out with a sentence we had recently learned in English class:

"I have some things to do!"

I fled, leaving the three men behind. I ran fast, as if sensing a danger.

This brief encounter would have passed without remark had Bob not come to find me again. I was out the next afternoon, and when I returned to my dorm, Zhang stopped me at the door of our building.

"That American came with Li to look for you," Zhang said, handing me a note. "He looked quite disappointed at not finding you here."

The note, written by Li, asked that I meet Bob at the foreign guesthouse at CUST for dinner. I was reluctant at first, but curiosity got the upper hand. It was strange enough that the foreigner had walked up to me the previous day after his lecture; it was stranger still that he had now found his way to my dorm. I wondered what had piqued his interest in me.

At the appointed hour and place, I met Bob, who had two friends with him, a white woman and a Chinese man. After dinner, we toured downtown Chengdu on our bikes, while the sky got darker and darker as night fell. Bob's friends were looking for a place to dance. There were many commercial dance halls in the city, a new trend in the "reform and opening-up" era, where for the price of a cheap ticket, one could dance the evening away. At each door, we heard tango or waltz music, and saw flickering shadows moving on the walls inside, but we were always blocked by the door guards: "Foreigners are not allowed!"

Oddly, something seemed to echo from half a century before. A popular story goes that, in the 1940s, many foreign countries' concessions (enclaves occupied and governed by foreign powers) in Shanghai had a sign at the entrance that read "Chinese and dogs not allowed!" This sign, equating Chinese with dogs, was the strongest insult imaginable in our country, proof that the foreigners understood something of Chinese culture.

Was tonight a belated revenge for that time? In the entire downtown of Chengdu, no exception was permitted. While Bob's two friends walked ahead, anxiously looking for the next dance hall, he lagged behind with me. Growing up in mountainous Chongqing, I had poor bike-riding skills. Soon,

Bob was riding beside me, shoulder to shoulder, shielding me from the heavy bike traffic on his side of the street.

On our bicycles, Bob and I conversed in my broken English and his pidgin Chinese, an intelligent and humorous conversation that would change my impression of Americans forever.

Many years later, when I read the American journalist H. L. Mencken's noted essay "On Being an American," I could not help but be amazed at how the author's general depiction of Americans matched perfectly my first impression of Bob: "They are, by long odds, the most charming people that I have ever encountered in this world. They have the same charm that one so often notes in a young girl, say of seventeen or eighteen, and perhaps it is grounded upon the same qualities: artlessness, great seriousness, extreme self-consciousness, a fresh and innocent point of view, a disarming and ingratiating ignorance." That was a portrait of Bob.

In retrospect, it was love at first sight, despite politics, despite nationality, despite myself. But I wouldn't admit it. I did not trust my instinct. A classical dogma I'd adhered to from birth, whether I realized it or not, was to be a diehard.

We did not find a dance place that night, and the next day Bob flew back to Shanghai, where he was teaching. He had only been in Chengdu for three days during the entire twenty-eight years of his life, and he had met me.

Two months later, in June, I went to Shanghai to attend the International System Dynamics Conference, which Bob had helped organize, on the campus of Shanghai Mechanical College. One night after dinner, Bob and I went for a walk. Climbing a small hill covered with privet bushes, which seemed to be the only green place on campus, I, at first, thought we were alone. A while into our conversation, however, some slight but discernible rustling sounds led to my discovery that, hidden behind every bush on the small hill, was a couple kissing. I was stunned.

Before I had recovered from my discovery, a new couple climbed up the hill. They paused briefly when passing us; I could feel their inquisitive eyes. Even in the dim light, a foreigner, especially with Bob's big puffy beard, was easy to distinguish. Did they think I was dating an American? I began to panic.

At that moment, Bob said, in a clear, calm voice, "I love you."

"But you are a foreigner!" I burst out.

"I am a man. You are a woman," he said, a bit surprised by my reaction, with his charming ignorance of my crisis.

What he had just said was a genuine shock. For the first time, I became aware of the sharp difference in our way of thinking. Growing up Chinese, I had always placed political identity ahead of gender, ahead of person. He was himself, but I had not been me.

And that was the turning point in my beginning to separate individual identity from political identity—the country, the race, or the religion.

We married a year later, after a long and winding underground courtship that disrupted Bob's planned trip to Tibet, and after my parents had gradually altered their view of him from that of an abstract, undesirable American to a dear person, a handy young man who could fix their broken shower head and leaking sink.

And now, over twenty years later, we are still happily married. Once I asked Bob what had caused him to walk up to me that first day in the auditorium, and he said, "When I looked out into the audience, I saw an interesting face in the back. You captured my imagination."

So that was how I became an American, and a writer in English.

Freddy Lucks Out

By Reggie Maxwell

Both my parents were natives of England. I was born in 1917 during a bombing raid by German zeppelins while my father was serving as a pilot with the Royal Air Force in North Africa. When World War I ended, my parents decided to try their fortune, first in Toronto, Canada, and then in Detroit, Michigan.

Listening to my father's stories about the "romance of the air," I developed a love for airplanes at an early age. My youth was spent reading and dreaming about flying. I made models, both rubber band and gas powered, and spent hours flying them in the summer skies. I couldn't wait until I was old enough to get into the "flying business." I majored in aeronautical design at Cass Technical High School in Detroit and decided that when I graduated, I would try to get a job in one of the many airplane factories in the Detroit area.

However, like most displaced Englishmen, my parents wanted to go home. Although they had a host of friends in the States, they had both left large families, whom they missed more with each passing year. After my grandmother died in England, my parents decided that they should return to live near their families. Notwithstanding that I was nineteen, and it meant leaving all my friends and interrupting my education, we returned to England in the mid-1930s.

My father, being an American-trained production engineer, soon found a position with a large company, making heavy forgings and pressings. I continued my schooling in Aeronautics at the Polytechnic Institute and, for a period, at Christ Church at Oxford, before getting a degree in Aeronautics from the University of London.

I was working in Research and Development with Omes Ltd. in Barnes, and I had an arrangement with the management that when my berth came up in the fall, I would be free to join Andley Pages, a major aircraft factory in Cricklewood. Pages was one of the finest aircraft companies in England.

After British Prime Minister Neville Chamberlain returned from Munich in 1939 and gave his "peace in our time" speech, we knew it was just a matter of time before we would be at war with Germany. Therefore, a number of us from the Polytechnic Institute volunteered to join the Royal Air Force as technical officers. As my specialty was aircraft design, I would be assigned to Farnborough, the RAF research station, if and when war broke out. However, the RAF research group did not have facilities ready to receive the required personnel, so I was only away from home for two weeks while I attended a preliminary orientation program. This would save time if hostilities broke out and I was called to serve.

Hitler moved into Poland, and war was declared on September 3rd, 1939. I was called into active service on the tenth, receiving my commission and being posted to the Royal Air Force research division at Farnborough, where I spent the remainder of the war.

Three of us who had been students together at the Polytechnic Institute arrived at Farnborough the same day: Reggie Bicknell, Freddy Dennet, and I. Reggie opted to room with a senior technician he knew, leaving Freddy and me as roommates.

Freddy and I had been in a number of classes and lectures together over the years, and always finished within a place or two of each other in our final examinations, but we ran with different crowds.

Freddy's preference was anything having to do with politics, while I had attached myself to a group whose interests were the arts, photography, and traveling around the countryside. However, once we had settled in, we found we had a number of common interests and became fast friends.

With usual military efficiency, the wind tunnel group received a requisition for two technical officers with the rank of flight lieutenant for dispatch duty. We had heard of this "special duty." It entailed the officer reporting to an airbase, where he received a top-secret envelope and was promptly put on an airplane to be transported to a prearranged destination. After he delivered the envelope he rested, if necessary, and then returned home.

I had heard stories of carriers who had been sent to parts of the States or Canada and had spent this "rest time" enjoying freedom from the war with excellent food and accommodations.

Freddy and I were selected for this special duty. We both had the same education, time in the shops, and experience in and around aircraft. Our assignments were placed in a hat, and we drew for the proposed journeys.

I drew Australia, and Freddy got the Americas. I tried to reason with him that, as neither of us had ever been to Australia, it didn't make any difference which of us went "down under." But, as I had grown up in Michigan, and I knew Americans, I was sure that once I arrived in America and explained the situation to them, they would somehow manage to snafu my visit enough to allow me to get to Detroit and see my friends. Finally, after I had promised him some of my ration points, Freddy agreed. We switched assignments, packed for a few days, and reported to the designated airfield.

That afternoon I took off with other RAF officers and Royal Navy personnel in a Wellington Bomber. I knew from its profile that it was equipped with extra fuel tanks, and that since it was only lightly armed, we were not flying into a war zone. Our destination had to be the east coast of the United States.

By watching the stars, we knew we were flying west. After a few hours, we landed somewhere for fuel; we guessed Iceland. Then, after many more hours in the air, we landed again. This time we were allowed to de-plane to stretch our legs. While the plane was being refueled, we were brought hot food and beverages, but we were kept isolated from the hangars and the barracks.

Once we were airborne again, heading south, we began speculating as to our final destination: New York, Florida, a Caribbean island, or a rumored research laboratory in Brazil. We finally fell asleep, and it was dark when the airship touched down onto a concrete strip. We gathered our gear and disembarked.

There were a number of Jeeps with American GIs waiting for us. An officer called my name and I climbed into one of the vehicles. As we drove, I tried to find out where we were, but the driver kept the conversation to mundane subjects. We arrived at a small building that had sentries at the door. They presented arms (they didn't have to, as my rank did not rate it), and I was ushered into the commanding officer's quarters. I pulled up into a salute and gave him the envelope. I felt rather glad that we didn't have to give passwords and counter passwords, as I was sure I would have felt like a bloody fool. He returned my salute, and, as he took the envelope, said, "Lieutenant, there is a canteen down the hall where you can get some food and a rest while waiting for your return flight."

"Return flight?" I cried. "I don't even know where I am—to return from."

The colonel smiled. "As you are not going on anywhere, it doesn't make any difference where you are, does it?"

I had something to eat, and although I tried my best, it was impossible to ascertain whether the airfield was located in the States, or if it was even in North America. The personnel, some of whom were pilots, questioned me about the war over England and in Europe. I told them what they wanted to know about the existing aircraft and losses, both the RAF and the American 8th Air Force. I was hoping they would trade information with me. But before they could say anything, my name was called, and I was winging it back, I assumed, to England, with dreams of spending some time in Detroit rapidly fading with each drone of the engines.

On the other hand, Freddy did not return immediately from Australia, and it was weeks before we heard the reason. The Air Ministry had decided that an aircraft plant was to be built in Australia to assemble and build certain types of light aircraft that were required in their theater of the war. This program was intended to ease up the difficulty of flying aircraft from either the States or England. The RAF insisted that a technical officer be in charge of the operation. When the search was made for this officer, it was found that Freddy was the only trained technical officer in the country.

Therefore, Wing Commander Freddy Dennet was now put in charge of this new operation.

Freddy held that position (with a raise in rank) until the fall of Japan and the end of the war. However, after the halt of hostilities, the Australian government did not want to lose this new aircraft industry with the many jobs it provided, so they managed to have the operation sold to a newly-formed private company.

It was an obvious move at this point to ask Freddy, who had managed the plant all during the war, to assume the position of director of the project.

Freddy's rank during the war, coupled with the influence he had due to his position in the factory, allowed him to meet all the families of the "social set" in western Australia. The first year after the war, he married the daughter of a family that owned a department store, something like Selfridges on Oxford Street in London. Working together, Freddy and his new father-in-law acquired many small businesses, both retail clothing and small engineering works, all of which were successful—making Freddy a very rich man.

After the war, when I had decided to return to America, I was clearing out some old papers and found Freddy's wedding invitation. I had to laugh at this turn of events and could not resist writing to him. I had not seen him since we had traded assignments and he had ended up in Australia at my behest.

He was happy to hear from me, and reminded me that his success in Australia was due to me insisting that we trade assignments that day that seemed so long ago. He offered to pay my expenses to move to Sydney and assured me of a well-paying position in one of his establishments. I declined his most generous offer, telling him I had accepted a position with an aircraft factory in California.

Reggie Maxwell retired in 1987 from an engineering company in Detroit, Michigan, where he was Vice President of Research. His lifetime interest in flying having waned, he now spends his time pursuing his interest in photography and writing short stories and novels for the reading pleasure of family and friends. "Freddy Lucks Out" is an excerpt from his unpublished book *Mitch.* He lives in Huntington Woods, Michigan, with his wife, Marva.

A Star Is Watching

By Abha Iyengar

It was raining in Delhi that afternoon when the call came. Our telephone was out of order, so Uncle Rahman called us at the upstairs neighbor's apartment. A call at the neighbor's meant that I had to take it. My husband, Vinod, and his father were at the office, and my mother-in-law could not run up the stairs fast enough.

"Hi, Uncle!" I yelled above the din made by the pelting rain and the neighbor's washing machine, which seemed to be on the verge of breaking all sound barriers with the racket it was making.

"Hullo, Abha," he said. "I can't get through to Iyengar and Vinod at the office."

"All the lines seem to be down!" I shouted.

"Well," he said, "do you remember the writing project you and Vinod worked on for my book?"

"Yes," I answered, a sudden excitement gripping me. Our writing on "Population" was published as part of a two-volume book edited by Uncle Rahman, who previously had been Advisor on Science Policy to the government of India and was now Director of the National Institute for Science, Technology and Development.

"The Technical University in Berlin wants one of you to present a paper on 'Urbanization and its Effect on Population' at a three-day conference there. Your air travel from India will be reimbursed, and lodging arrangements will be made for you. I will be presenting a paper, too. You and Vinod decide which one of you will go. It is in December sometime. I will give you the details later."

"I'm going," I replied. "I will get back to you, Uncle. And thanks."

I could barely contain the excitement bubbling within me. I am a rather diffident person. I find all kinds of excuses for not doing the things I really want to do. Until then, I had immersed myself in taking care of the kids and the family. I had convinced myself that for the moment, this was all I wanted. However, one thing was definite. If anyone was going to Berlin, *I was.*

On Vinod's return from the office, I told him about Uncle's call. He was all for it. He knew that I had studied some German during my college years, and that the language and people fascinated me. I had always wanted to visit Germany. This was a Heaven-sent opportunity.

I began, in earnest, researching and writing the paper on urbanization. After submitting the draft to Uncle Rahman for evaluation, I then rewrote it and gave it the final touches. I had never presented a paper on my own, but that did not deter me. The fact that my children were just four and six years old, and I would be leaving them behind, did not daunt me either. Vinod had said he would look after them, and it was only a matter of a few days. Moreover, my mother-in-law was there, and I had a servant to take care of chores. The greatest opposition came from my mother-in-law. She did not like the fact that I would be leaving the children behind, or that I would be traveling alone. I had anticipated her response; usually I succumbed to pressure, but this time I dug my heels in.

At the same time, I was developing a touch of a cold. I went to the local doctor, who prescribed some antibiotics, but the medicine did not help. I was losing my appetite at the sight of food. Silly fool that I was, I was thrilled at the idea of losing weight and looking more "hip" in my jeans. I ignored what was really happening to my system and put it down to stress and last-minute jitters.

My kids were also acting up (they could sense the tension around them), and my mother-in-law was still trying to dissuade me from going, telling me I was not well enough to travel. Vinod, seeing how pale I was, also tried to convince me to cancel the trip, though he knew I was hell-bent on going. I refused to budge. My Taurean temperament had come to the fore. Once he knew I would not change my mind, he supported me all the way, making things as easy for me as he could.

Hence, it came about that I flew to Berlin to attend the three-day conference. After the conference, I planned to holiday with another uncle who was going to be in England at that time and had offered to show me London for two days before I returned to India. On the second day of the conference, however, after successfully presenting my paper, I immediately became so sick that I had to be hospitalized.

It was discovered that I had Hepatitis A. The doctors believed that I had picked up the infection in India, but it had manifested itself while I was in Berlin. I was rushed to the Krankenhaus Prenzlauer Berg, the largest liver treatment hospital in Berlin, where I went into a coma that same night.

I learned later that the German doctors had called Vinod and told him, "Come now if you want to see your wife's face one last time." He flew to Germany immediately, with my father arranging for his ticket and ten American dollars in his pocket, loaned by a relative. Vinod could not get any money exchanged because he already had gone to America earlier that year on a work-related visit, and the Indian law at that time did not allow an individual to take foreign exchange out of the country more than once a year. However, nothing on earth was going to stop Vinod from being with me.

When my distraught husband landed in Germany, a friend of my younger sister's husband was there to meet him. Jurgen did not know Vinod, but he not only came to the airport, he also offered to allow Vinod to stay at his home as long he wished. Jurgen came to the hospital the next day with chocolates and a large card that opened up into a beautiful cutout. It showed a famous building in Berlin and a star over it, with "A star is watching over you" written in his lovely calligraphy. He had come up with this overnight, for me, a woman he was meeting for the first time. Why should a stranger do so much? Only a sense of humanity and compassion drives gentle souls like him. He is a dear friend now and forever.

It was the team of able East German doctors at the Krankenhaus (the Berlin Wall had only recently fallen) who saved my life. They did it without doing a liver transplant. They half-jokingly said that mine was an Indian liver, stronger than a European one, and so they were able to revive it. The fact was that they had to keep me alive until the papers for a liver transplant could be completed, which took longer because I was a foreigner. By the time the paperwork was done, I was already on the way to recovery due to the doctors' relentless efforts, and I did not need the liver transplant after all.

How the doctors pampered me! I was their star patient. My recovery was a miracle, which even they were unable to fully comprehend. My three-day odyssey to present my paper at the conference turned into a month-and-a-half long stay in Berlin. Then, weak and frail, but bubbling with the spirit of Christmas and the New Year, which I had celebrated with new friends with whom I felt a special bond, I was ready to go home.

On my return to India, I was so weak that Vinod arranged a wheelchair for me at the airport. The sight of my family, especially the kids, made me forget everything else. As they ran forward to hug me, my eyes filled with tears. The children had been well looked after while I had been away. They now clung to me, unwilling to let go.

This separation from my family had been a necessary one, willed by the grace of God. People say that if I had stayed back, rested in India, and not taken the strenuous journey to Berlin, I would have recovered quicker. I know differently. I know I was destined to go.

My reasoning is simple. Though I was not feeling quite up to par, I did not think that my condition warranted "special" attention. The local doctor had said that I had a simple cold and had prescribed antibiotics, which I took—a terrible thing to do to an ailing liver, I found out later! My eyes and skin did not have the yellowness that indicates jaundice. Since I did not know that I was suffering from a major illness, I would not have rested had I stayed home in India, but would have continued attending to the demands of house and family until it was too late. A relative of ours, a successful doctor, told me later that if I had been hospitalized in Delhi in my critical condition, I would not have survived. Although India has some of the world's best doctors, no hospital in India had the necessary special drugs or medical equipment to revive my liver. No liver transplant had been successfully done in India.

It was Fate that made me receive the call that rainy day; Fate that caused me to accept the offer; Fate that ensured I was where I could get specialized medical care. Fate sent me to present that paper in Berlin so that I could live. I am a firm believer in Destiny and Karma today.

Jurgen said, "A star is watching over you."

Oh, yes, my friend, you were so right!

Abha Iyengar is a writer, poet, scriptwriter and amateur photographer. Her work has appeared in print and online in India and abroad. Her writing has been published in several *Chicken Soup* series books. She has contributed to *Gowanus Books, Insolent Rudder, Arabesques Review, Citizen 32, M.A.G, Breakaway Books, Dead Drunk Dublin, Nothing but Red,* and other literary journals. She holds creative writing workshops and does performance poetry. She writes Urdu poetry as well and has made a poem-film titled *Parwaaz* that is being shown in international film festivals. Her website is www.abhaiyengar.com.

Twister of Fate

By Jan Johnson-Tyler

Sometimes an hour of Fate's serenest weather strikes through our changeful sky in its coming beams.

Bayard Taylor

I had only six weeks to hire a highly-specialized employee for the multi-million dollar project I was running for a large software company in Silicon Valley. I needed someone who was conversant in an arcane type of computer language used most frequently for technical documentation. If I didn't find this employee in six weeks, I would lose the requisition to hire someone. If I didn't hire an employee at all, the project was at high risk of failure, and my career could be over.

Because the extremely small number of people who knew this language worked for the government or government contractors, I frenetically started recruiting these sources nationwide. After interviewing one dud after another, I finally found a great candidate. She and I talked at length on the phone about her credentials and the job, and we were both excited. I wangled permission to fly her out from Oklahoma for a personal interview, something my company rarely allowed.

When Barbara and I met in person, we immediately hit it off. She knew the material cold, was intelligent, and funny. With blood-red fingernails, jet-black hair and punk jewelry, she was not at all what I had expected from Oklahoma. She was perfect in every way for the job, and I told her so. However, since the job would necessitate a move, she would need to discuss it with her boyfriend. We agreed to talk again the middle of the following week.

Barbara called me as promised, but not with the news I had anticipated. She had talked to her boss candidly about her new job prospects, and her boss had offered her a huge raise and a management position in response, something she'd never expected. It was the job she had always wanted—her dream job—and she had, of course, accepted it. She wished me luck with my search. I was devastated.

The time flew by, and I was about to run up against my deadline. With only two days left to hire someone, there was no one even interesting enough to interview. I had used every recruiting tool I could think of—contacted every organization, attended tradeshows and job fairs, talked to recruiters, and checked Webster's, a job placement service on the Internet. I was out of options.

Then I thought of Barbara. Maybe she didn't like her new job, but didn't feel comfortable enough to call and tell me. It seemed highly unlikely after two short weeks, but I thought I could cover up my brazenness by saying I was calling to see if she knew someone whom she could recommend for the job. I made the call and asked her how things were going, how she liked her new job in management.

"I hate it!" she told me, flat out.

"Enough to leave?" I asked.

Without a second's hesitation, she responded, "When can I come out?"

She and her boyfriend moved to California one week later. She loved the job, loved the environment, and was thrilled that she and her beau had made the move. She was a dedicated worker, wowing everyone with her knowledge and savvy. It was a perfect match, and we were both very happy. We joked about how fortunate it was for both of us that I had dared to call her back on a whim.

One day about two months after she started working with us, I was surprised to see her waiting by my office door when I arrived at work. I was an early bird, and she usually arrived much later. She looked shaken. Her red eyes made it clear that she had been crying.

"Thank you for saving my life," she said.

Confused, I joked, "Why, was the job that bad?"

"No, you don't understand. I just talked to a friend who lived down the street from me. A twister hit my old neighborhood early this morning, and leveled our old apartment building in Oklahoma. Everyone was killed."

We were both very thankful that I had acted on my impulse to call her two months earlier.

Jan Johnson-Tyler is a neurodiversity counselor, providing career, vocational and transitional services to older adolescents and adults who have autistic spectrum disorders, learning differences, attention deficit disorders, and pervasive mood disorders. She is a single mom to two great kids and lives in the San Francisco Bay Area.

Grandmother Spirits

By Mary-Alice Boulter

Fate means seeing the hand of God move clearly through your life, even with your eyes closed.

Rusty Fischer

I rushed toward my front door, running late for actors' call, as the telephone rang.

"Hello?" I picked up the receiver, glancing at the clock.

"Hello, this is Dr. Holmes, your dad's doctor."

My breath caught in my throat.

"You asked me to call you when he reached the final stages of his illness. I saw him late this afternoon. He has perhaps a month or six weeks to live. Do you have any questions?"

The questions had already been asked a hundred times; the answers were unchanging.

"No," I responded, taking a deep breath. "No, no questions. I'll be in touch once I've thought things through. Thank you." I hung up the telephone slowly.

This was it; finally, after two and a half years of knowing what was coming. I wanted to sit down and absorb the news, to compose myself and then call my father. I looked again at the clock. No time. Our show was due to start in a little over an hour, and I should have been there already.

"The show must go on," I told myself with a new understanding of the old show business maxim. I allowed myself one quick sob, then fled to my car.

It was August 2nd, opening night of the "Days of Old Fort Hall," an outdoor historical pageant. The drama, which told of the founding of the original Idaho fort in fur-trapper days, was the culmination of months of script research, auditions, travel back and forth between town and the Fort Hall Indian Reservation, and long evenings of rehearsal with more than a hundred people. We had been working toward this night for a long time.

I was the narrator, The Storyteller, a primary role, so I had no option but to report in. As I drove, my mind was still on the telephone call and its ramifications. My feelings were hundreds of miles away with my father.

I soon arrived at the replica of the historic fort that loomed in the slanting sun like a ghost out of Idaho's past. Flanking it on either side were two tipi encampments. One encampment represented a Shoshoni village of Sacajawea's people. It teemed with sturdy brown men and women in traditional dress, shining horses, even a dog or two playing with the scampering children among the tents and campfires.

The other grouping of lodges echoed with the raucous laughter of mountain men in buckskin outfits and fur caps, knives and long-barreled black powder rifles at their sides. They jostled each other and practiced throwing tomahawks against the huge tree stump propped up at the edge of their clearing.

The villages were replicas, but both the native and the mountain man populations actually lived there for the duration of the final rehearsals and the shows. There are several organizations of mountain men who regularly hold rendezvous around the country. They live in their tipis or lodges and are very particular about everything being as authentic as possible, in dress, custom, food, lodging and activities, depicting the period, roughly, from the 1830s to the 1850s. Though full tribes don't do it anymore, there are still some Native Americans who follow the plant and animal resources to gather for food, clothing and many other uses.

Therefore, both the Shoshoni and the mountain man encampments were indeed authentic, if only for a short time. Tipis were set up, they cooked over open fires, tended to their horses and children, and of course slept there at night. Even though they were set up around a replica of the original Fort Hall, they were functional living situations. One couple even got married there!

I parked my old Volvo and went to find Joyce. Joyce was Shoshoni-Bannock, and we had become good friends after working closely together on the pageant. I found her backstage.

Joyce took my arm and steered me behind the set, among some trees. "What's wrong?" she asked.

I told her of the telephone call. "Right after the final show on Saturday night, I plan to drive up to Washington to see Dad. I need to go to him!"

"Of course you do. You belong with him at the end. Does Jeff know yet?"

My son, Jeff, was somewhere in the Far East. I didn't know where exactly—either Japan or Korea. He'd talked his way aboard a cargo ship embarking from Seattle to tour those exotic countries and to "find out a little more" about himself and his birthplace.

"No. I don't know how to get in touch with him. I have a tentative contact person in Kamakura, and will try to call her. But who knows when he'll be in touch with me? Oh, Joyce, I want so to talk to Jeff about this!"

Joyce held me close. "We'll figure something out; don't worry. You just go and get ready for this show, my sister." She gave me a gentle push toward the dressing area.

I wiped tears from my cheeks, then wandered up to where the horses were tethered. I patted the neck of a vibrant young pinto gelding whose forelock was decorated with an eagle feather. Red painted circles around his eyes and hand prints on his flanks gave him an owly, otherworldly look. I forced myself to be calm, stroking the pony, talking softly to him.

Finally, I was ready. The actors were all in their places, and as the opening music surged, I walked out on the huge outdoor stage to the microphone, awash in a bright circle of light, and began to tell the story.

Opening night excitement was high and contagious, and the show went well. Applause rolled across the green and onto the stage as the finale soared and the lights dimmed. It was over.

I was almost carried off my feet as the keyed-up players swarmed backstage, whooping and chattering in glee. Even the animals felt it. The horses tossed their manes as they pushed and nipped at each other and at the dogs dashing underfoot.

I worked through the melee, looking for Joyce. She found me and touched my shoulder. "Come. Emma wants to talk to you."

Emma was one of the elders, proud and wise, a deeply spiritual woman. She traveled each year to the International Peace Conference, wherever it was held, and added her prayers for universal peace to those of people from around the globe. Emma was waiting by the campfire at her tipi.

"Joyce told me about your problem. Come here; I will pray for you." The old woman held out her hand, and I took it.

I sighed. "Oh, Emma, I'm so worried. I need to talk to my son, but I don't know how to find him."

"Don't worry. I will pray for you to the grandmother spirits. You stand here near the fire and face the east."

The diminutive woman with weathered face and long gray hair placed one hand lightly on my shoulder. She began to pray, chanting a gentle swift song of oddly familiar words, reminding me of Japanese language rhythms I once knew. The halting melodious cadences rose on the air toward the full moon suspended in the sky. The fire beside us flickered and flared, sending sparks to follow the prayers, carrying them to their destination as they rose higher, to be lost in the small night sounds.

Emma finished with her head held high, chin raised and eyes closed. Her lips silently formed promises of things to come. Then she sighed, opened her eyes and cast a satisfied look at me.

"Okay, it's done. You go home now and sleep. You look terrible. I'll see you tomorrow night."

I thanked Emma with a swift touch on her cheek. Joyce walked with me to my car.

We stepped carefully in our moccasins among the tipis, avoiding gear, sleeping dogs, children's games and lodge poles. I was surprised at how quiet the village had become. The prayers must have lasted longer than I realized. Families were bedding down in their lodges; fires were only embers now. Soft murmurs of adult conversation drifted quietly from darkened door openings. Occasionally, a horse would stamp or snort. In the shadows under a tree, a dog yipped in dream pursuit of ghost prey.

At the Volvo, Joyce turned to me. "Emma knows what she's doing. Try to sleep tonight. She's taking care of things. I'll see you tomorrow."

The performances on Thursday and Friday nights went equally well. As I was ready to leave for the final performance on Saturday evening, the telephone rang. I hesitated, then answered.

"Hello?"

"Mom—it's Jeff!"

"Jeff! Where are you?"

"Hiroshima …"

"Hiroshima? I didn't know you were going there!"

"I wasn't. But when I got to Japan three days ago, I remembered what you said about Hiroshima and the part of the bombed-out city they kept as a Peace Park—what an impact it had on you the first time you saw it. So I decided to come here and see for myself."

I couldn't speak.

"Mom, are you still there?"

"Yes, I'm here."

"Well, I arrived in Hiroshima a little while ago, and it just happens to be the anniversary of the bomb …"

"Of course! It's August 5th here, but with the International Date Line, it's the sixth over there!"

"Yeah, and I happened to show up just at the beginning of the three hours when the city allows any foreigner to make a free three minute telephone call to anywhere in the world. So I got in line, and here I am. Isn't that great?"

"Oh, honey, you don't know how badly I needed you to call!" I started to cry.

"Mom! What's wrong?"

"Dr. Holmes called three days ago. Your grandfather has perhaps a month, maybe six weeks to live."

"Oh, wow." I could hear the catch in his voice.

"Jeff, I wish you were here!"

"Oh, wow," he murmured again. "I need to think about this. The next guy in line wants to make his call. I promise I'll call you by Monday and let you know what I'm going to do. I gotta hang up now."

"Okay, honey. I'll wait for your call."

I replaced the receiver with a hand that trembled so badly I had to steady it with my other hand. I took a deep breath and hurried out the door.

As soon as I arrived at the village, I ran to find Emma. I found her smoke-tanning deer hides over her campsite fire.

"Emma, Emma, it's working!"

The handsome old woman looked at me intently. "Tell me. How is it working?"

In a rush of words, I related the story of my son's call, then stopped and looked at her. Emma studied me silently. She suddenly grinned.

"Of course it worked! That's the third time this month!"

Jeff traveled back to spend the last month of Dad's life with him. Dad died in our arms.

Mabel's Dream

By Janice Baylis

This is a case of not being in the wrong place at the wrong time. The year was 1959. Mabel and I were both teachers at Castaic Elementary School in Castaic, California. I lived thirty miles south of the school in Burbank, so I took my three sons to the school in Castaic. Mabel lived even farther away in Glendale.

After Mabel had major surgery, she asked to meet me partway each morning so she didn't have to drive all the way to work. We began meeting at seven o'clock in the corner of a small strip-mall parking lot and leaving her car there. Early one morning, before I left my house, Mabel phoned.

"I feel bad about taking up space in that parking lot all day," she said. "Will you meet me around the next corner? I'll leave my car on the residential street."

"Okay by me," I agreed.

As Mabel was getting into my car at seven that morning, we heard an enormous CRASH! Driving back by the parking lot, we saw a small, private plane, a Funk. It had crashed, upside down, in the corner where we would have been at that very moment had Mabel parked her car there that morning.

"How did you know, Mabel?" I asked.

"I dreamed it last night," she replied. "But I didn't want to tell you it was a dream. I thought you might think I was silly to pay attention to a dream. And I didn't know if it would really happen."

"Thank God you acted on it," I said.

"Wow!" said my son Brad from the back seat, which was exactly how I felt.

In 2004, when I heard the Los Angeles area television news report an airplane crash off the runway of Whiteman Airport, it immediately triggered the thought that the crash Mabel dreamed about must have been in the newspaper. So I did a search on the Internet and found the local paper for 1959 was on microfiche at the Norridge University Library. I went to the library and found an article about the crash in Mabel's dream. It was reported on October 22, 1959, in the *Van Nuys News.* My three sons, who had been with me in the car at the time of the crash, were very interested to see the newspaper article forty-five years later.

Mabel's dream experience launched Janice into a lifetime of self-directed and academic study of dreaming. Later, she taught dream study at a community college and authored books telling what she had learned about dreams. Today she is considered an expert on dreams. She is currently working on another book, which is about how the dream-mind chooses the images it uses.

The Angel That Couldn't Fly

By Michael T. Dolan

Fate touches us all. We cannot turn a blind eye to the connections of the cosmos.

The greatest mystery of the universe no longer remains a mystery. Why did the chicken cross the road?

There were five of us in the rusty passenger van that day. We had looked forward all summer to our vacation at the end of August—an extended weekend camping trip at Virginia's Shenandoah National Park—before our respective universities called my friends and me back to the classroom.

We wanted to get on the road as early as possible that Thursday afternoon to savor every bit of Shenandoah sun that we could. My original plan of action was to clock out of work at three p.m., pick up Dave, Skooter, Ed, and Eileen by 3:30, do some quick grocery shopping, and be cruising north on I-64 by four o'clock.

The drive from our hometown of Richmond to Shenandoah doesn't take much more than two hours, which would leave us with plenty of time to set up camp before the sun called it a day.

Just after two o'clock that Thursday afternoon, however, an hour shy of my quitting time, the feeder on our main printing press went out. If the project we were working on hadn't needed to be finished that day, I would have been more than happy to begin the weekend an hour early. Deadlines are deadlines, though, and as pressman for the day, I had to wait around for some techs to get the press back up and running. By 3:30, the press was feeding properly, and I was able to get back to work. I finished the job almost two hours late.

Leaving work at about 4:30, I hit the beginning of rush hour, which further delayed picking up my by-then irritated friends. It wasn't until after 5:30 that we pulled out of Bill's Grub & Gear and were chugging north on I-64 in my '91 Ford van. On the radio, Kenny Rogers sang "You got to know when to hold 'em, know when to fold 'em, know when to walk away, know when to run ..." Our vacation had begun.

After an hour and a half of driving, heading northeast on Route 33, we all felt close to our destination. We didn't need the sign, "Shenandoah National Park—16 miles," to know we were almost there. We could feel it. Treetops thickened, blocking out what little sunlight remained in the sky. The road shoulder narrowed, disappearing as we began to ascend the Blue Ridge Mountains. With the ascent, my van began to show its age, but did its best to navigate the winding road at a top speed of thirty-five miles per hour. Finally, we were aware of the last sign that civilization was behind us: the radio succumbed completely to static. Just as it did—just as I began to turn off the power button—Eileen screamed, "STOP!"

Without knowing the reason, I instinctively pounded the brake pedal to the floor and throttled the steering wheel with a vise-like grip. After a few feet of screeching tires, the van came to a halt. The five of us also stopped short, following the lurching lead of centripetal force.

My heart was pounding; adrenaline coursed through my body. Chills ran down my spine. It took a moment for me to come to my senses and discover what Eileen had seen that I hadn't. A chicken.

Yes, a chicken.

And, yes, it was crossing the road.

We all stared at it in absolute amazement as the chicken, less than five yards in front of us, walked calmly toward the other side! It was steadfast in its resolve to accomplish this simple task and gave no indication that it realized how close it had come to becoming a messy fixture on my van's front grill. Static came from the radio as I gazed at the bird, wondering what in the heck a chicken was doing some three thousand feet up. In the Blue Ridge Mountains, no less.

As I continued to stare, a light began to glow from around a curve in the road twenty yards ahead of us. I soon realized it was the headlights of a logging truck speeding around the bend. In our lane!

I laid on my horn. There was nothing else to do; the time to react was gone. My heart seemed to stop beating. I realized with horror that the trucker's time to react was also gone. He would hit us dead on, crush the van and kill us all on impact. Then the truck would send us through the guardrail and down the embankment, where we would be buried at the bottom of the mountain.

At the last possible moment, the truck swerved across the double white lines and back into its own lane. The entire van shook as the logging truck barreled past us at such a speed that I was certain that its brakes must have given out.

After it had passed, it took a moment for me to realize that we were still alive. All of us remained in shocked silence, the only sound being the static from the radio. Had that chicken not crossed the road at that very moment, I certainly would not be writing this. Instead, the van would have continued on its journey and met the grill of an oncoming semi just as we turned the bend. The chicken saved us the ghastly fate of becoming road kill.

Questions entered my mind and refused to leave. They still do. Why was the logging truck speeding down the mountain in the wrong lane? What was a logging truck doing on Route 33 anyway? Taking the scenic route out of Shenandoah National Park? Did the driver miss the sign that read "DOWNGRADE NEXT 6 MILES: USE LOW GEAR"? What would have happened if the driver hadn't steered his rig back into the right lane? What if I hadn't stopped for the chicken?

I got out of the van. I could barely stand. With shaking legs, I placed my left hand on the van to keep my balance. It didn't work. I fell down to my knees on the asphalt road. At first I didn't believe my eyes. It couldn't be!

But it was. Lying next to me in the middle of the road was a feather—one single white chicken feather. Suddenly, it all made sense to me. Why did the chicken cross the road? I now knew the answer to that timeless mystery. So did Eileen. And Dave. And Scooter. Even Ed, who somehow managed to sleep through the entire miracle. We should know the answer. After all, we witnessed it. Why did the chicken cross the road?

To save us.

I don't remember much about the rest of our vacation. That's just as well. The drive there was the important part.

Yes, angels do have wings. Some of them just come in different forms.

Michael T. Dolan is a writer from West Chester, Pennsylvania. His essays have appeared in newspapers and magazines across the country. He is the author of the novel *Walden,* a satirical look at a young man's search for his own identity. *Walden* was published by Conversari House in 2006. Visit www.conversari.com to read more from Dolan.

The Sapphire Ring

By Katherine O'Neal Kimsey

When I look back over my long life, if there is one thing that leaps out at me, it is the role of luck and chance in our lives. From this particular string of accidental happenings all the rest followed.

Katharine Graham

It was the early fall of 1938. I was living with my older brother, Walter, and his wife, Blanche, in Canton, North Carolina. My parents died when I was very young, and I had lived most of my life with Grandma in Staffordtown, a section of Copperhill, Tennessee, but she had agreed that I could live with Walter and Blanche while finishing high school. Grandma was eighty-two, too old to be raising a teenager.

I was in my junior year of high school, about to turn sixteen in November, and I was like all the other teenage girls I knew. We went to church three times on Sunday—morning church, Sunday School, and evening church—where our main interest was boys. They flirted by winking and smiling at us when we were supposed to be listening to the preacher or engrossed in Bible studies. It was different then than it is now: I was very sheltered, and flirting was not expected to lead to anything more than holding hands.

At some point, Blanche's nephew, Beryl Hall, started walking me home from church on Sunday evenings. He then surprised me with a sapphire ring, which Blanche decided was an engagement ring when she spotted it on my finger. She became very upset because Beryl was twenty-four years old, and she thought he was much too old for me, and that I was too young to get engaged, anyway. I tried to tell her that it was only a friendship ring. She wouldn't listen to me. She telephoned my older sister Bonnie in Tennessee, and said I was about to marry a twenty-four-year-old man. I had no intention of marrying Beryl, even if he had asked me, which he hadn't, but Blanche got Bonnie upset, too. Bonnie was fourteen years older than I was, and very protective. She wasn't about to have me marry a twenty-four-year-old, so she rushed down to Canton from her home in Turtletown, packed me up, and took me back with her. I didn't have a chance to even say goodbye to Beryl.

I did not want to go back to Tennessee with Bonnie. Turtletown was in a rural area north of Atlanta, Georgia, and I did not want to live out in the country. I loved Canton. I cried bitterly when Blanche insisted that I leave with Bonnie, and I vowed to return as soon as I could. I even left my favorite dress at the home of a woman I had babysat for, telling her I would be back for it. I wished with all my heart that I had never accepted that sapphire ring.

In Tennessee, my life turned out to be much like it had been in North Carolina. We still went to church three times on Sunday, and the boys flirted with the girls. I was the new girl in town, and all the boys told me how pretty I was. I could have my pick of them, with one exception. The handsomest one of all, twenty-year-old JD Kimsey, who was six-foot-two with a muscular build, black curly hair and deep brown eyes, pretended to ignore me. However, I could tell he was interested by the way he looked at me, and I sure was interested in him. The problem was that JD was engaged to Helen Hensley, a match that had been arranged by their families. I became engaged to his cousin, Jake Dale, just to spite JD, although I had no intention of marrying Jake.

Then one night, Fate, which I now see brought me back to Tennessee in the first place, took another turn in my direction. I was angry at Jake Dale because he went out celebrating our engagement with the boys, and was drinking beer, and forgot about a date with me. He was trying to get back in my good graces as he walked me home from church along the country road leading to Bonnie's house. I kept telling him to go away and leave me alone. We were right in front of the Kimsey house, which was set somewhat back from the road. It was very dark, and we didn't know that JD was sitting on the porch, listening to us argue.

Suddenly, JD stepped out of the shadows, took Jake by the arm, and told him to leave. He said, "I'll take Katherine home." Jake turned on his heel and stalked off.

JD walked me to Bonnie's house, and we sat on the porch swing, talking until almost midnight. He told me I was beautiful, and that he had fallen in love with me the first time he saw me. I asked him why he had never paid any attention to me, and he said he figured that when I got done with the rest of the boys, I would get around to him. JD said he would break his engagement to Helen if I would break my engagement to Jake. I told him I already had; that was why Jake and I were arguing.

That night was December 7, 1938. On a cold, rainy night, a little over a month later, January 17, 1939, JD and I eloped across the Georgia state line in his old Ford. We had the Justice of the Peace who had performed the marriage ceremony of a girlfriend of mine, and a witness he provided, sitting in the back seat of the car so they couldn't see, in the dark, how young I was. JD and I repeated our vows from the front seat, with rain seeping in through the car roof. We went to a movie afterwards.

Whoever married JD Kimsey was fated to live a different kind of life than the other girls in town. By a stroke of luck, it was I. We ended up living all over the world, having many different experiences in different cultures before JD retired. That's not to say that things were always easy. When we got married, the country was still reeling from The Great Depression, and it was hard for a young man to get work. JD had only a high school education, plus a couple of college business courses, taken by correspondence. He got work in a saw mill at first, and then did farm work for a dollar a day.

Shortly after our first child, Brenda, was born in February 1940, JD heard that Utah Construction Company was hiring men for a tunnel job in Andrews, North Carolina. JD made thirteen trips to Andrews, trying to get hired, before Ben Arp, the project manager, gave him a job operating a drill. JD didn't know how to drill, but his father told him what to do, and he was a foreman within three months.

We had had two more children, Carolyn and Robert, by the time we moved permanently from Tennessee the summer of 1946. We then lived in the western part of the United States while JD worked for Ben Arp on various underground construction jobs. Ben promoted him to general superintendent in 1948 when he went to work on a tunnel project for Utah Construction in Bingham Canyon, Utah. In 1951, our last child, Richard, was born in Salt Lake City.

In 1956, Ben Arp called JD and said FASMA, a French-American company, was looking for someone to oversee the completion of a dam and underground power station as part of the Snowy Mountains Project in Australia; that they were so far behind, they were about to lose the contract. He had recommended JD for the job. A Frenchman came to Salt Lake City to negotiate with JD, and a deal was struck.

After that, we spent over twenty years living in foreign countries, while JD worked as the project manager on various jobs. We loved Australia the most. We lived there for twelve years on three different assignments. The Australian people were very friendly to Americans. We met Prime Minister Robert Menzies when he came to visit the job site, and I helped give a tea for his wife, Dame Pattie. We entertained the French ambassador and other dignitaries.

While managing an important project when we lived in New Zealand, JD appeared with Prime Minister Keith Jacka Holyoake on the cover of *Photo Review,* a New Zealand news magazine. By then, JD had a reputation as one of the top underground construction men in the world. We also lived in Greece and Chile, and JD traveled to other countries in the course of his employment.

As is customary in the construction business, JD's company paid all of our housing expenses when we lived overseas. They paid first-class airfare or ship accommodations for us when we traveled between the United States and foreign countries. They paid for our vacation trips home. When local schools were not adequate, and it became necessary to send our two youngest children to board at a private high school in the United States, the company paid for this as well.

JD and I faced heartaches and tragedies over the years just like every other couple, but all in all, we had a wonderful life together, and we ended up financially secure in our retirement from his hard work. The example he set influenced our children, all of whom became successful adults.

If it had not been for Beryl giving me the sapphire ring, and Bonnie coming to Canton to take me back to Turtletown, I would not have met JD, and I would have missed a great adventure. My daughter Brenda asked me recently what happened to the ring and Beryl Hall. I still had the ring, and wore it some, even after JD and I got married, but it was stolen many years ago. It truly was only a friendship ring as far as I was concerned, and Beryl Hall never did get married.

Katherine O'Neal Kimsey is an artist of still-lifes and landscapes. She lives in Salt Lake City, Utah. She enjoys writing poetry and received a Golden Poet Award from the *World of Poetry* in 1988 for her poem "The Torrent," written under her pen name Ramona See. Katy, now a widow, says she still misses Australia and other countries she lived in when her husband, JD, worked on overseas jobs.

Mother's Voice

By Garnet Hunt White

I grew up "on the fence," as we say in the Missouri Ozarks. Some people believe in extrasensory perception. Others dismiss it with bemused tolerance or persecution. Many families in my community still believe in haunted houses and "bright, round moving objects high up in the sky." Most look upon these people as odd. I wonder, are they?

My father was a farmer who traveled around investing in livestock and real estate. Many times I heard him say that his subconscious, or intuition, often warned him not to travel, or told him to buy or sell, or not to buy or sell, and the advice turned out to be right.

Are we so set in our ways that we can't understand or accept anything except what can be seen by the naked eye, or recorded on tape by the human voice?

I had an experience that will always be a wonderment to me.

My mother had a stroke and could not talk. My father kept her at home and had nurses with her around the clock. He also hired a speech teacher to work with her.

My husband, Glenn, and I lived a hundred miles to the east of my parents' house. Three times a week, after the school bell rang at three p.m., I left my classroom and drove to Doniphan, Missouri, to be with Mother, and try to keep up her morale.

Teaching school and traveling a hundred miles to my parents' home three times a week, and then driving the hundred miles back to our home in Cape Girardeau, meant that I was always short of sleep.

One evening in May 1983, I bid Mother goodbye, hugged my father, then headed the car back home to meet Glenn.

I had been on the road about an hour. Suddenly, Mother yelled "Garnet!" and I awoke. The car was headed straight for a bridge rail and pillar. I slammed on the brakes and swerved the car away from the railing. I stopped. My hands shook on the steering wheel. My feet trembled on the floorboard. Shivering from head to foot, every organ inside me yo-yoed up and down. I stayed parked for what seemed like an eternity.

Where had Mother's voice come from? It had been in the car. How did she know I had gone to sleep? I had left my parents' home an hour before.

Was I hearing Mother's voice from my subconscious mind? How come she yelled at me just as my car was heading for the bridge? I had fallen asleep. Mother's voice had awakened me. I was scared; frightened that I had almost hit the bridge, and shocked at hearing her voice.

When I got home, I telephoned my father. The first thing he said was, "Your mother spoke. She called 'Garnet' and sat up in bed. You had been gone about an hour."

That was right around the time I almost hit the bridge!

Through chattering teeth, I told him about falling asleep while driving, and how Mother's crying out had probably saved my life.

Father told me he had had many experiences in his life when some unknown power had warned him of danger. He told me about some of the incidents, and that began to calm me, but I still had not regained my composure. I asked him to tell Mother that I had heard her call my name.

When I got home, I told Glenn about hearing Mother's voice and said, "You probably don't believe me."

"Garnet, I believe you," he said. "I could tell you of many incidents during World War II when the men in my squadron heard unknown voices or felt an unknown power. The reason I've never mentioned these things before is because many people aren't ready to hear about extrasensory powers."

My talk with Glenn helped relieve some of my tension. I didn't fully comprehend how I had heard Mother speak. From the time she had her stroke until she died fifteen months later, my name on that near-fatal day, was the only time anyone heard her speak.

A Fate beyond my control decided what was to happen to me that day. After that, I was humble when I heard people speak about "strange" happenings in their lives. This occasion made me give credence to guardian angels and heavenly spirits.

I was in danger; Mother's voice saved me.

Garnet Hunt White is a retired schoolteacher who wrote stories using her pupil's names as characters in order to encourage them to read. Garnet has been published in two anthologies, *Stories for a Woman's Heart* and *Chocolate for a Chocolate Lover's Heart*. Several of her stories have won awards, and she organized the Ripley County Writers Guild in Missouri, where she lives. She also loves animals, as did her late, wonderful husband, Glenn.

The Rowboat

Anonymous

A man was stranded in his house in a flooded area, and a rescuer came by in a rowboat. "Get in," he said.

"No," the victim replied. "I will wait for God to save me."

Then, as the water got higher, he climbed up on the roof of the house.

A rescuer in a motorboat came by and said "Get in."

"No, I will wait for God to save me." Then, as the man clung to the edge of the chimney, a man in a helicopter came by. "Get in," he said.

Again the man said, "No, I will wait for God to save me."

The man perished in the flood and went to stand before God.

"God," he asked, "why didn't you save me?"

God replied, "I sent you a rowboat, a motorboat, and a helicopter. It was you who chose your fate, not me."

The Sisters

By Brenda Warneka

A white BMW rounded the curve in the night darkness, its headlights catching the silhouette of two Standard Poodles running into the road. The driver was not going that fast, but a screech pierced the air as he hit the brakes; then a sickening thump sounded as the car pulled to a stop, too late.

As soon as my husband, Dick, let the poodles out of the van at the large, grassy field used as a dog park, they sprinted off in a direction they had never gone before. Thinking they must have been frightened by something they had heard, he started after them, but the black dogs blended into the dark of the rainy Thanksgiving evening.

As Dick ran, he called their names, "Chien! BonBon!" The dogs suddenly circled back into an area lit by a pair of street lamps, then darted into the road, quickly cutting back onto the grass, then heading into the road again, their long legs propelling them into the path of disaster.

Dogs are allowed to run free at the Coronado Cays park, and although it is unfenced, Dick had thought the poodles were safe unleashed because they were familiar with the area, and were usually very well-behaved. The Cays was their favorite place to play when we were staying at our condominium in

Coronado, California. Dick would leave the side door of the van open, and the dogs would run back and jump in when they were ready to go. We were in Coronado now for the long Thanksgiving weekend, our last visit for the year. We had finished a turkey dinner with our neighbors half an hour earlier, and it wasn't that late, but dark descends early in the wintertime in Southern California.

Dick thought at first that both dogs had been hit by the car, but as he ran toward them, he saw only Chien, the male, lying on the ground. The driver and passengers were climbing out of the BMW. One of the passengers, an older woman, started to cry. BonBon, the female, was prancing in circles in the road. Dick grabbed her by the collar and pulled her into the van. He then rushed to Chien, who was badly hurt and in shock.

As Dick gingerly lifted the fifty-two-pound dog into the van with the help of a passerby who had been walking his own dog, Chien, crazed with pain, sank his teeth into Dick's hand, resulting in an injury that took weeks to heal. Chien had never bitten anyone before. Dick drove to the nearest animal hospital. BonBon, frightened and shaking, crouched in the front wheel well of the van while Chien died in the back.

Dick, BonBon, and I each grieved in our own way over Chien's sudden death. Dick broke down and cried twice. I kept remembering Thanksgiving morning when Chien pawed at me, begging for attention while I worked at the computer, and how I had shooed him away. Now I wished I had kissed him and told him how much I loved him.

BonBon was traumatized. She lay on her dog bed, staring straight ahead for hours at a time. Chien was already a member of our family when three-month-old BonBon had come to live with us six years before. They had formed an instant bond, never thereafter being more than a few feet apart. They were extremely loving dogs, both toward each other and toward us.

Late Saturday night, we drove from Coronado to our home in suburban Phoenix. As we pulled into the driveway, BonBon became very excited. When we let her into the house, she ran from room to room, searching for Chien, sniffing and smelling his scent. When she did not find him, she took to her bed with one of her stuffed toys, or "babies," and rarely left the bed, day or night, except when she needed to go outside.

For years, BonBon and Chien had relished an early morning routine in our backyard of barking back and forth with the dogs next door. Fortunately, no other neighbors were close enough to be disturbed. Our property has a block wall around it, but if the poodles crouched down, they could peer at their pals through an opening under the wall where a wash runs between the two lots.

Now, when BonBon went out in the morning, she stood by silently while the dogs on the other side barked; she didn't even get down to look under the wall anymore. She ignored her favorite treat—Trader Joe's peanut butter dog cookies. And when we got home from work (in the past, a joyous occasion with the poodles jumping up on us, barking and licking us), she stayed on her bed. It was very sad to see our previously happy-go-lucky BonBon, the dog that we always joked had a spring inside her, in this terrible state of depression.

Within a few days of Chien's death, Dick and I knew we had to get another companion for BonBon. For various reasons, we didn't want to start over with a puppy, so we decided to get another dog about BonBon's age. Chien normally had been such a well-behaved dog that we called him "The Little Gentleman." But he had had one bad trait: he disliked little dogs. He barked ferociously and pulled at his leash when a small dog walked by. We preferred to avoid what we considered to be "macho" behavior, so we agreed to look for a female, and we definitely wanted another black Standard Poodle.

We started our search for a six-year-old, black female Standard Poodle by contacting animal shelters and poodle rescue leagues over the Internet. We did not find any Standard Poodles that needed a home, let alone a poodle of our specifications, although we contacted places as far away as La Jolla, California. Apparently, it is very unusual for a Standard Poodle to end up at an animal shelter or rescue league, and the breeders we talked to had only puppies.

A whisper of Fate stirred in my mind at some point during our search, reminding me that the breeder in El Paso, Texas, who sold us Chien and BonBon, had said when we left the kennel with BonBon, "If anything ever happens and you can't keep your dogs, call me, and I'll take them."

I reminded Dick of this and said, "Maybe she told other people that, too, and someone has brought back a poodle we could have." He didn't pay much attention at first, but when we found no Standard Poodles closer to home, he finally looked up the breeder's name and called to see if she had any ideas about where we might find the dog we were looking for.

Brigitte Copeland had very sad news to impart. Her only daughter, a partner in her business, had died, and she was in the process of closing down Copeland Kennels after twenty-six years in business, to go home to Germany to take care of her aging parents. She remembered both Chien and BonBon well. Chien had been the runt of his litter—too small to show—but she had planned to use him for obedience trials until we bought him when he was nine months old. Six months later, when Chien's mother was pregnant, we ordered a female puppy (BonBon) from the upcoming litter. Now Brigitte had several Standard Poodles for which she needed homes before she left for Germany, including three females named Maggie, Lucy, and Angel, who were between the ages of six and eight years old. Brigitte asked about BonBon's personality and said she would think about which dog might be best for us.

When she called back two days later, she suggested that BonBon might get along well with Maggie, a retired show dog. Maggie was a six-year-old, black female Standard Poodle, *exactly* the dog we had been searching for! In fact, Fate had made sure there could not have been a more perfect companion for our dear, sweet BonBon. The dog named Maggie was BonBon's own littermate. *Her sister!*

We flew to El Paso on December 18, 2002, to pick up Maggie, almost six years to the day we had made the same trip to pick up BonBon. Maggie is an American Kennel Club "finished champion," whose formal name is Champion Falkirk Hocus Pocus. She has had one litter of six puppies, two of whom are finished champions. She comes from a litter of six—two being finished champions as well. While BonBon was living the life of a common pet, hanging out in our backyard with Chien, her sister Maggie was strutting around the show ring to the applause of the crowds. And while BonBon, spayed at an early age, had mothered stuffed toys, Maggie had nursed real pups.

When we put a collar around Maggie's neck to attach the leash to lead her from the kennel to our rental car, Brigitte told us it was the first time in Maggie's life she had worn a regular dog collar; that a show dog doesn't wear a collar because it will wear down the fur around its neck. Brigitte demonstrated how, when she wanted Maggie to do something, instead of pulling on her collar, she led her by the ears.

Dick drove the rental car from El Paso to Phoenix with me sitting in the back, tightly hugging Maggie. We arrived home in the early evening and took Maggie and BonBon into our backyard to introduce them to each other. They sniffed one another and got acquainted while on leashes, then were let loose. They were standoffish, but everything seemed to be going fine, until BonBon did a fast run around the yard and "body slammed" Maggie.

The body slam was a signal that BonBon was ready to play—it was something Chien used to do to BonBon when he wanted her to chase him. Maggie, who obviously had never been body slammed before, turned up her nose at this somewhat crude behavior and started to walk delicately back toward the house, walking straight into the swimming pool.

Maggie had never lived at a place with a swimming pool, so she didn't know that she couldn't walk on water. As soon as her front paws got wet, she realized what was happening, caught her balance and backed up, walked around the pool and into the house, holding her nose high in the air.

Maggie's grooming put poor BonBon to shame. Maggie was coal black when we picked her up, even though Brigitte had described her to us ahead of time as having some grey in her hair, and BonBon was clearly greying. Maggie had a fairly simple poodle cut, not the fancy cut she would have enjoyed before she retired from the show ring, but she did sport a wonderful puffy pompom tail with a little ring shaved at the base of it, and cute little black toes stuck out from her shaved feet. BonBon had still a simpler cut and was overdue to be professionally groomed. I immediately got out a brush and started working on her.

At bedtime, BonBon lay down on her bed in our bedroom, where she sleeps next to a very large, floppy, stuffed bunny we bought when she was new at our house to give her a "mother" to cuddle up to at night. She stretched out her legs and strategically placed her front paws on Chien's bed, next to hers, to keep Maggie off should she decide to sleep there. But Maggie was not interested in sleeping on a dog bed. She was uneasy her first night away from the only home she had ever known, and she spent the night on the floor next to Dick's side of the bed. We wondered if she had ever slept anywhere but in a kennel.

We took the poodles on leashes for a walk in the neighborhood the next morning. Maggie held her head high and glided along as though she were in a show ring. BonBon, harking back to her German ancestors, ran alongside the road with her nose to the ground, sniffing for game. Quite a contrast! We had to leave the dogs alone during the day while we went to work, but since they were ignoring each other, we were sure they would be okay while we were gone.

Dick came home from work early that day and took the dogs to the grocery store in what we call "the dog van," purchased specifically for the poodles. Chien and BonBon loved sleeping on the back seat, looking out the side windows or lying on the floor between the captain chairs in front and being petted as we traveled along. Maggie apparently had never ridden in a vehicle except in a cage, so she was a little confused about what to do. She chose to lie on the floor—and traveled along, facing backwards.

Over the next few weeks, BonBon's depression disappeared, and Maggie's assimilation into the family became complete. Maggie was just as loving as Chien and BonBon had always been. The sisters became close friends, licking each other's faces in unison, running together to the wall in the backyard to bark at the dogs next door, and playfully taking turns sleeping on each other's beds. BonBon gave up body slams, perhaps because she was learning more dignified behavior from her refined sister. For our part, we bought some professional "Black Star" color enhancing shampoo to take to our dog groomer, after which both dogs pranced around in coal-black coats.

Chien's death was the result of bad Fate, or being in the wrong place at the wrong time. If Dick had not taken the poodles to the Cays that night or had kept them on their leashes, Chien would not have died as he did. If Dick had arrived with the dogs at the park five minutes later, and the dogs missed hearing whatever it was that caused them to take flight, or if the BMW had not happened along just when it did, things might have been different. Chien might be with us today.

We also had good Fate, however, in that we found Maggie because we had called Brigitte when we did. If we'd called even a few days later, Maggie might have been sold to someone else, and a few weeks later, Brigitte would already have left for Germany, and the phone would have been disconnected. The two sisters, together at birth and then separated, were reunited six years later in middle age to live out the rest of their lives together—due to Fate.

A Life-Altering Twist of Fate

By Katia Gusarov

In December 1941, in the city of Simferopol in the former Soviet Union, Tatiana Zelenskaya, a singer, and her husband, Pavel Chariuta, the musician who accompanied her, were young actors performing together on stage. The city was already under Nazi rule when one of the theater employees approached Tatiana with a request that would save a life and forever change the lives of the young couple.

The employee, whom Tatiana would later realize had heard of the German plans via his connection with the municipal underground, asked if she would take in and hide a Jewish child. He informed her that in just a few days, all the Jews in the city would be gathered in one location prior to their deportation. At the collection point it would be possible, in the general confusion, to "kidnap" a few children, and by so doing, save them, he confided.

In spite of the danger, Tatiana agreed, and on the appointed day and time, she stood in a nearby alley leading to the designated collection point of the Jews and waited. After some time, a stranger appeared leading a little girl with black, curly hair and big, frightened eyes by the hand. The woman handed her charge to Tatiana, who walked home with the child through the city's alleys and backstreets. As Tatiana took off the little girl's coat, a note, with the child's name, address, and date of birth fell to the floor.

From that day on, four-year-old Luba Kogan lived in Tatiana and Pavel's home. At first she was sad, refused to eat and constantly asked, "Where is my mother?" Weeks passed and slowly, Luba's memories of her past life faded and were replaced with new impressions, until one day she referred to Tatiana as "Mother." It was not long before Tatiana and Pavel became extremely attached to Luba and could not imagine life without her.

Although it was illegal to harbor a Jewish child and the neighbors were well aware of Luba, not a single one of them questioned her origins or disclosed her presence during the two years and two months of the war.

Years later, when Tatiana herself was questioned as to whether she was frightened to hide a Jewish child, she replied, "I was young. I did what I felt I had to do. My parents told me that I was jeopardizing myself, but my husband supported me."

Following the war, the couple attempted to determine the fate of Luba's parents. Through the Kogan family's neighbors, they learned that Luba's mother and brother had been executed and that her father had died while serving on the front.

In 1947, a man who introduced himself as a representative of the Jewish community approached the couple with an offer of monetary assistance towards Luba's care. Tatiana and Pavel refused for fear that if they accepted aid, Luba would be taken from them.

Luba continued to live with the couple well into adolescence without knowing that Tatiana and Pavel were not her biological parents. In 1953, when Luba was sixteen years old and was required to obtain an identity card, Tatiana finally told her the true story of her childhood, and only then did Tatiana and Pavel officially adopt Luba.

In 1965, when Luba was already married and herself a mother, a coincidental meeting resulted in a startling turn of events. Luba's husband, a taxi driver, met another taxi driver, an older man, with a story to tell. As the younger man listened to the details which seemed to match the details of his wife's life, he came to the uncertain but intuitive conclusion that this man might be Luba's biological father, who until then had been presumed dead in battle.

As it turned out, after the war, when Itzak Kogan, Luba's father, returned to Simferopol following his service in the Red Army, his neighbors informed him that his wife and his two children had been killed. Overwhelmed by his loss, Itzak could not continue to live in Simferopol and therefore moved to Krasnoyarsk in Russia. In time, Itzak remarried, started a new family, and began working as a taxi driver.

Following this encounter with Luba's husband that seemed more miracle than sheer coincidence, father and daughter were reunited in an emotional meeting that was reported by the local newspaper.

Many years later, following the deaths of both Pavel and Itzak, Luba brought Tatiana, the woman who had saved her life and adopted her as her own child, to live with her. In 1993, one of Luba's sons immigrated to Israel with his family. While visiting Yad Vashem for the first time, her son learned of Yad Vashem's Righteous Among the Nations Department and told his mother's story to its staff members. In 1995, Tatiana Zelenskaya and Pavel Chariuta received the Righteous Among the Nations designation at a ceremony at Yad Vashem.

During the ceremony, Tatiana recalled the bittersweet twist of fate in a hushed voice, and with tears in her eyes, said: "I remember that fall evening in 1941 when fifteen thousand Jews were murdered and how happy I was that I was able to save one life—that of a little girl who is standing next to me today— my beloved and only daughter."

That same year, Luba, her family, and Tatiana Zelenskaya immigrated to Israel where they are still living together today.

Katia Gusarov emigrated from Russia to Israel in 1990. She became acquainted with Tatiana Zelenskaya and her adopted daughter, Luba, through her work for Yad Vashem, which is a huge complex outside of Jerusalem dedicated to the memory of the Holocaust. (See www.yad-vashem.org.ll.) Katia works for the Righteous Among the Nations Department, which is dedicated to gathering information and honoring non-Jews who rescued Jews during World War II at the risk of their own lives. A mother of three, Katia maintains friendly relations with Tatiana and Luba.

Some Kind of Miracle

By Arlene Uslander

Everything comes gradually at its appointed hour.
Ovid

My mother had been in a deep sleep for three days, taking in no food at all, and a minimum of forced liquid. A "Do Not Resuscitate" sign hung over her bed. Every time I looked at the sign, I shuddered. The finality of the words chilled me, even though the heat in her bedroom was way too high.

She was eighty-eight years old and had reached the end of a long illness. She was still in her own apartment, but I had arranged for around-the-clock nursing care for her; I did not leave her side during those three days. On the fourth morning, a Sunday, I called my husband and asked him to pick me up and drive me home (some forty minutes from my mother's apartment) so that I could get clean clothes. I had been wearing the same pair of jeans and blouse for four days, having had no idea when I arrived that the end was so near.

As we drove home that Sunday, my husband and I decided that before we went back to my mother's apartment, we would stop at the funeral home to make arrangements. The doctor had said that she would not last more than a few days at most, and the previous evening, the visiting nurse had agreed with his prognosis. We felt it would be better to make the funeral arrangements while we were still relatively calm, rather than after the emotional trauma of death had set in. I also wanted to stop at the grocery store so there would be some food in the refrigerator for the nurses and myself.

Once at my house, I quickly showered and dressed, then threw a few clothes into a shopping bag. We got back into the car. Suddenly, I told my husband that I had changed my mind about stopping off at the funeral home. I did not want to take time to buy groceries, either. Something inside me told me that we had to get back to my mother in a hurry—before it was too late.

I rang the bell in the lobby and the daytime nurse, Callie, buzzed me in. After the elevator ride up to the twenty-second floor, I saw Callie at the end of the hall, a look of amazement on her face. "It's some kind of miracle!" she exclaimed. "Your mother's eyes are open!"

Hurrying into my mother's bedroom, I was shocked to see that her eyes *were* open. She was propped up in the rented hospital bed, staring straight ahead. At first I thought she was dead, and my heart started racing. But then she shifted her gaze and looked straight at me. She had a puzzled, questioning look on her face, as if to ask "Where am I?" Or perhaps "Where am I going?"

Then a grimace passed over her face—a grimace that I have replayed in my mind over and over again. Was it a grimace of physical pain? Of fear? Of sadness? I think by then she felt no more pain, so it must have been a combination of fear and sadness—deep sadness at leaving, and fear of the unknown. She needed the comfort of being in my arms when she began her journey.

I held her frail body gently and spoke to her softly, telling her how much I loved her. And then I could feel and see that she was gone.

I asked Callie how long my mother's eyes had been open before I arrived.

"Only a few minutes," she said. "When I heard you ring the bell downstairs, I said to your mother, 'There's your daughter. Now you just hold on there. Don't you die before she gets here.' And she *did* hold on. She waited for you."

Thinking about the fact that something had told me not to stop for anything on the way back to my mother's apartment, but to hurry as fast as I could; thinking about the fact that my mother had opened her eyes when I rang the bell, and kept them open until I got there, so that I was able to say goodbye to her, I suspect that Callie was right. It *was* some kind of miracle.

Cowboys and Indians

By Lakshmi Palecanda

Take a woman who is the ultimate extrovert, a romantic and exceptionally impractical woman in daily life. Try pairing her up with an extremely reserved man who is intensely independent and eminently practical. What will you get? A marriage that is well-rounded yet interesting, a union where the bills get paid in spite of underlying chaos, a garden with beautiful flowers blooming alongside prosaic beans and squash. In other words, my marriage.

This union of opposites did not happen without glitches.

In 1991, I arrived in the United States from India with a scholarship to study for a master's degree in Biology. Having been brought up in a very sheltered family with traditional Indian values, I was eager to experience a different culture, but woefully ill-equipped to deal with the drastic changes I would have to make.

I was addicted to cowboy movies, and so when confronted with a choice of universities, I chose Montana State University in Bozeman, Montana, where I thought I would meet cowboys. It never registered in my mind that this was not going to be like going to see a Clint Eastwood film, where I would go back home in a couple of hours, eat my mother's wonderful curries, and be nice and warm every day of the year. I arrived in Montana in March to foot-deep snow, bone-deep cold, and soul-deep silence. I stayed indoors out of the snow as much as I could, cranking the thermostat up to near-volcanic temperatures, but there was nothing I could do about the quiet. Only a person who has lived amidst the cacophony that is India will truly understand the problems I had in adjusting to the lack of street sounds that I faced in small-town USA.

The other problems I had were in no way trivial either. I didn't know how to cook, and I was a vegetarian … in beef country! I also did not know a soul in Montana. Luckily for me, there was a small Indian community, comprised mostly of students at the university, who met me at the airport and showed me around.

As my new "friends" were introducing me on campus that first day, one man, also from India, turned and walked away without bothering to meet me. I was hurt by this display of bad manners, and immediately disliked him. Later, he was introduced to me as Aiyappa, a Ph.D student in Immunology. This time, I got even; I chatted away "nineteen to the dozen" (British expression often used in India) with the others and pointedly ignored him. He seemed irritated by my silliness.

Our paths crossed again three weeks later when Aiyappa brought me some of my mail that had been delivered to his department by mistake. Since I was very homesick at the time, I overcame my dislike of him enough to be somewhat friendly, and we discovered we had several things in common. We spoke the same languages, we liked the same music, we lived close to each other in India—and he was quite good-looking, too! Apparently, Aiyappa thought the same of me, for we began seeing each other, quite casually at first, but more seriously as time went on. This brought up several issues.

The first was that I had an understanding about a future marriage with a friend in India. This informal pact had been made more out of my desire for a family rather than any romantic feelings, but it had to be dealt with honestly. Once it became clear to me that my relationship with Aiyappa was no casual friendship, I wrote to my friend in India asking to be released from our pact. He agreed, and I was free.

As for the love of my life, if circumstances had been different, Aiyappa would have been married to someone else by the time I had met him. In 1990 he had gone back to India with plans of entering into an arranged marriage, as most Indians do. But even as his sisters stood ready with lists of eligible single women, he decided against it due to some problems with his educational program. By the time I entered the picture, he was back in this country, the problems had been resolved, and he was still free!

We began dating in the real sense of the word three months after our first meeting, and Aiyappa proposed marriage four months later. I accepted joyfully, and we entered part two of our problematic relationship.

Though we are both Indians and Hindus by religion, we came from cultures that are vastly different. My family is lacto-vegetarian in its food habits and non-alcoholic on principle, whereas in Aiyappa's family, meat is part of the everyday menu, and no occasion is considered complete without alcoholic beverages being served. Even the dress of my husband's culture is different. However, both families had one thing in common: they did not approve of us marrying outside our communities.

They expressed their disapproval indirectly. We probably didn't know our own minds, they said. We should wait for maybe two years before getting married, just to be sure. Both of us loved our own families too much to view estrangement from them without sorrow, so we waited, working on our educational projects. In the meantime, our families tried to dissuade us from tying the knot, but it did not work.

Aiyappa and I were engaged October 17, 1991, and we were married October 18, 1993, exactly two years later. We had three wedding ceremonies: a civil ceremony at the local Law and Justice Center in Bozeman, followed by two ceremonies in India, one in accordance with each of our family's customs. Both families graciously attended the two ceremonies in India in full force, although they still had qualms.

In the years since that day, despite ups and downs, our union has been stable, strengthened over the years by the birth of our two beautiful daughters. Our families have become friends, and our children revel in the rich traditions of both cultures.

Of course, early on in our relationship, I asked Aiyappa why he had turned and walked away from me the first day we saw each other. He explained that I was with a group of people who tended to be very garrulous, and he had to be at work within a very short time, so he thought it better to leave rather than get involved in conversation that would delay his getting to his job on time.

As for our opposing temperaments, we have learned to complement each other instead of dwelling on our differences. I am very outgoing; he is very, very reserved. I am not exactly the neatest person in the world, and my head is in la-la land all the time; he is very organized both physically and mentally. I am an inveterate procrastinator; he is always ten minutes early. Our similarities: we both love our families, we are both very compassionate, and we both share the same sense of humor.

What God has taken so much trouble to bring together, no man should put asunder.

Lakshmi Palecanda is an Indian-American who lives in Bozeman, Montana, with her husband and two daughters. A student of plant science, she has a master's degree in Biological Sciences. After working in laboratories as a research associate for a decade, she has taken up

writing full-time. She is a columnist for an Indian-American magazine called *India Currents*, and also works as a freelance writer. She is currently working on a romance novel about an Indian adopted by an American family who goes searching for her roots.

Her Brother's Keeper

By Darryl C. Didier

I do not believe that the good Lord plays dice.
Albert Einstein

It was dusk, a beautiful evening. The setting sun filled the sky with streaks of orange and red. My girlfriend and I sat on a wooden bench overlooking the waterfall garden that was surrounded by pines and maples. The bench was on a fifty-foot ridge where the cascades began. The mood was perfect.

After an hour passed, we walked from the waterfall garden down the prairie grass slope. Then something very strange happened. On the way down the forty degree incline, my equilibrium became a little shaky. As we all tend to do, I denied any problem and hoped it would go away. I was floating on air anyway, without a care in the world. Good job; promising future; beautiful, smart girlfriend; my parents on vacation, and my older sister, Brenda, away at her weekend job. All kinds of exciting images danced in my head.

That night turned out to be the last night I was ever "without a care in the world," because at 11:30 p.m., long after I drove my girlfriend home, I awoke from a deep sleep with a severe headache. I ran downstairs to the kitchen and swallowed two Bufferin, thinking that was all I needed. Then I went down to the basement to rest on a cot, where I often sprawled out when I was under the weather, hoping the headache would dissipate. It persisted. I went back upstairs to the kitchen and called my friend Paul, who lived a few blocks away. Before I finished dialing his number, the headache became so severe that I curled up on the kitchen floor.

The next thing I knew, my sister, Brenda, was at my side. In a quivering voice, I told her of my problem. We lived only a few blocks from a hospital, so she called the emergency room and told them she was bringing me in.

Brenda was the head choreographer at a dinner theater, and that night she was conducting a rehearsal for the musical *The Best Little Whorehouse in Texas.* Opening night was just around the corner. Since the rehearsals often ran late into the night, Brenda usually took advantage of one of her perks, a rented hotel room, to avoid the late-night forty-minute drive home.

To make a long and excruciatingly painful story short, it turned out that my blinding headache, as well as the shaky equilibrium I had experienced earlier in the evening, were symptoms of a malignant brain tumor. Now, years later (thanks to extensive life-threatening surgery, and many, many prayers), I am cancer free.

My sister often recollects that on July 16, 1990, the evening of my admittance to the hospital, she was tired after the long rehearsal and was seriously considering staying overnight at the hotel. But a warning in her mind made her go home. She'd had a feeling that something was terribly wrong.

If Brenda had not heard and responded to that inner message, the doctors said I probably would have gone into a coma and died. I wouldn't be here to hug her today!

After undergoing a very complicated, life-threatening brain tumor operation, Darryl Didier lived for seventeen more years. Following a year of intensive rehabilitation, he became actively involved with his local chapter of the American Cancer Society by raising funds, and as a motivational speaker in grade schools, high schools, businesses, and even prisons, on the topic of cancer prevention, especially the dangers of smoking. He also taught Sunday school. His book, *Force a Miracle*, with a foreword by Mike Ditka, Hall of Fame football player, is an incredible inspiration to anyone who has a hurdle to climb, as was Darryl to everyone who knew him.

Swimmer's Delight

By Virginia K. Sparks

My hometown, Corning, California, roasted like a well-done chicken in hundred-degree heat that August morning. Dad had decided to go fishing on the Sacramento River, and we four kids were excited to accompany him. We would play at the swimming hole, known as Swimmer's Delight, while he fished. This was when I was eleven years old, many years before the Whiskeytown Dam was built and made the river too cold and deep for swimming.

Ten miles from home, we crossed over Woodson's Bridge to the picnic grounds and parked our car. Huge oak trees trailing long vines cast cooling shade over the picnic tables. We kids loved to seize a wrist-thick vine, and with a running start, swing out over the water and drop into the river with a huge splash.

Mom was adamant about doing our swimming before we ate. No one seemed too concerned about the river's current while we swam in the green water. Oh, what bliss!

We dove and swam all afternoon, coming out now and then to bask on the hot sand and rocks. The beach made a wide sweeping curve at that spot. From there I could see my dad, made smaller by the distance, standing in a rowboat borrowed from his friend Charlie Hansen. Earlier, I had seen Charlie visiting with friends in the park near the picnic tables.

Dad's fishing line made little rainbows of light now and again as he cast into the water. My mouth watered, savoring the thought of the eighteen-inch black bass we would have for supper. Dad always caught something.

My perfect day was shattered by two men on the bridge, hollering and waving their arms like crazy men, pointing down into the river. I could tell they were hobos by the packs on their shoulders: men who rode the trains from town to town looking for work, or maybe because they just wanted to roam. We kids had been strictly warned to stay away from them.

The hobos kept yelling and pointing until men lounging on the river bank stood up to see what all the commotion was about. Two of them dove into the river, their arms flaying the water into a froth as they swam, nearly going under the bridge. They came back, each stroking with one arm, towing a body between them. As they came ashore, we could see it was a boy, his arms dangling, his head hanging down, his feet leaving wet lines as he was dragged across the sand. His two rescuers rushed him to one of the picnic tables.

It was my nine-year-old brother Floyd! I was petrified until someone yelled, "Go get Mike!" Mike was my father. I set out, running barefoot across the hot rocks along the shore, my arms pumping up and down, my legs churning, jumping over knee-high rocks, until I was close to my dad's fishing grounds.

I yelled, "Daddy, Floyd drowned! Hurry! Hurry!" I cupped my hands and screamed at him over and over. I saw him throw down his rod, sit to grasp the oars and pull downriver with all his might. I ran back, but my dad beat me to the site.

When I arrived, out of breath, frantic with fear, Charlie Hansen lay on the picnic table, using his body as a log, while my father rolled and squeezed Floyd's body across Charlie's, over and over. As I watched Floyd's limp body being pummeled, all I could think of was that I had brought this terrible tragedy on our family because in my angry quarreling with Floyd that morning, I had yelled, "I wish you were dead!" Now he was lying motionless, making no response to the efforts to revive him. I wasn't aware of it, but Mom later said that I was crying and promising never to fight with Floyd or anyone else again if God would only let him live.

All at once, water gushed from Floyd's mouth, and he stirred. I don't recall what else happened, but I remember my brother sitting up, wheezing for breath while people around us laughed with relief and whacked my father on the back, everyone talking at once.

The two men who had rescued Floyd said that when they reached him, they had caught him by his swimming trunks just as he was going under a pile of brush at the river's bottom. Had they been even a second later, they would have missed him. The two hobos, looking down from the bridge, had seen Floyd drifting downstream with the current. Another fortunate thing was that Floyd's tongue had settled in the back of his throat, which kept the water out of his lungs. When my father used a finger to clear Floyd's mouth of debris, it loosened his tongue and enabled him to cough up the water he had gulped in.

In time, humbled and contrite, I looked unsuccessfully for the two hobos. I wanted to thank them for saving my brother's life by their persistent yelling and pointing. We never knew who they were, or why they were on the bridge that day. No one saw them again. I hope they know that they saved my brother's life.

I often wonder what would have happened if those two men had taken a different route. No one else was on the bridge that afternoon. Was it Fate that intervened?

Virginia Kennedy Sparks grew up in Corning, California, attending local schools. After moving to Humboldt County, California, she wrote historical pieces for the *Humboldt Times,* and later wrote a column on historical subjects for the *Humboldt Beacon.* Her writing has appeared in various magazines and historical quarterlies. Other interests include sewing, gardening and landscaping, collecting recipes from the 1700s and 1800s, photography and genealogy.

Pop's Angel Lounge

By Garnet Hunt White

When Pop remodeled our home, he added what each member of the family wanted—two extra bedrooms, an additional bath, a larger kitchen, a breakfast nook, a sun porch and thirty-two windows. However, after the renovation, one room in the middle of the house was left with no windows. We called it the "dark room."

When I was a child, chills raced up and down my spine every time I walked into the dark room. Who knew what could be hiding in the shadows? Vicky, one of my sixth grade classmates, thought she saw a ghost in the room. Two other friends, Stella and Ora, were afraid to go into the room at all. My parents built a new home the year I was married, and they decided to sell the house with the dark room. My husband, Glenn, and I bought it. We used the dark room only as a hall and never tarried in passing between rooms. I still thought of the room with apprehension.

Glenn's job took him out of town two nights each week. I stayed home with our dog, Rex. Late one night when Glenn was away, a rainstorm knocked out the power. Rex jumped on my bed and barked until I awoke. He then whined and ran around the room every time the lightning flashed or the thunder clapped.

I finally got out of bed and took Rex to the dark room. He felt safe there because he couldn't see the lightning or hear the thunder. As we lay on the floor, huddled together, I dropped off to sleep.

Rex suddenly started to yelp again. He tugged on my sleeve, bounded out of the room, ran toward the bedroom door, then back to me, only to repeat his antics.

What did I smell? What was that flashing yellow light? I stumbled toward the bedroom. Flames covered my bed! Lightning had run into the house and ignited the bed covers. I grabbed Glenn's pillow. Clutching it with both hands, I began beating out the blaze. Adrenaline was flowing through my body. I kept slamming the pillow against it, pounding until the fire was ash.

With the fire out, my body went limp. The storm still raged. I dropped to the floor and crawled back toward the dark room. Rex kept howling, but he nudged me along. Finally, sprawled on the floor in the dark room, I hugged him.

When the morning calmness came, I realized I had spent more time in the dark room that night than in all the times I had been there in the past.

I put breakfast on hold, petted Rex, and said, "Gotta call Mom and Pop to see if they're okay. Then I'll fix you some chicken strips."

A dead telephone. The storm had knocked out my phone line. I put Rex into the car to go to my parents' house. Before I even got out of the garage, their car pulled into the driveway.

I jumped out of the car and ran to them, jabbering and crying.

"Hey, hey!" Pop said. "Are you all right? I can't understand a word you're saying. Glenn called. Said he couldn't get through to you."

Grinning through tears, I embraced them both. Inside the house, I showed them the bedroom. Then, half laughing, half crying, I led them into the dark room to finish the tale of how Pop, Rex and the dark room saved my life.

"Oh, Pop. I'm so thankful to you for this room," I sobbed as he put his arms around me. "I'm alive now because of you."

Ever since then, I have had new respect for Pop's dark room. He had built an Angels' Lounge.

The Fate of Aspirin

By Rusty Fischer

When you turn the right corner, at just the right time, in just the right place, and meet just the right circumstances, person or event ... you come to know the true meaning of fate.

I wasn't even supposed to be there. I was graduating from college, and the gang at my second job, a local restaurant, wanted to throw me a congratulatory party.

"We'll meet you at the Raw Bar!" they shouted as I headed out the door with a tip-apron full of extra singles from an impromptu collection they'd taken up for me. "Don't be late!"

Of course, with my college-boy lack of a sense of direction, I went to the Raw Bar on the south side of town, even as they all sped directly to the north one. Now, a full hour later, and still nursing my lukewarm first beer of the night, I had finally realized the problem and gotten a bartender at the *other* Raw Bar to summon the most sober of the group to the phone. Needless to say, the party had been a roaring success, and none of them were in any condition to come and meet me.

I sat back down on my warm barstool and finished my beer. *Oh well, at least I won't have a hangover tomorrow.*

At that moment, the gorgeous teacher from the school where I had just completed my student internship walked through the door with a friend of hers. Embarrassed to be caught in a dingy bar all alone, I quickly turned to the bartender and ordered another beer.

Meanwhile, the long-legged beauty I had lusted after, day in and day out, strode effortlessly to a table for two and joined her friend for a pitcher of beer and some steamed shrimp. I watched from behind the camouflage of my three-hundred-pound biker barstool neighbor as the teacher's delicate hands alternately raised her frothy beer and peeled a still steaming shrimp.

How different she seemed from the consummate teacher who had often written me a "helpful" little note after witnessing yet another disastrous attempt on my part to lead my unruly fifth grade class quietly through the elementary school halls.

"If you divided your line in half," she had written in elegant script on floral stationary, "they'd be much easier to control. Sincerely, Ms. Richard." I'd saved every note and devoured them as religiously as I did my college advisor's halfhearted yet stern evaluations.

And now she was *here,* live and in person. My stressful senior internship, leading to my teaching degree, was over. There would be no more little notes from Ms. Richard. No more expert advice in the teachers' lounge while I secretly vibed her with sexy ESP and suggestive rapid eye movements. But it didn't matter anyway. My flirtations had gone unrequited, and the other bachelors at the bar already were making plans to swoop in on the two unescorted beauties and their half-eaten shrimp.

I slid a hefty tip across the bar and left without a word. The humidity in the warm Florida night air reminded me of the dull headache forming in the back of my weary head, and I drove my battered Corolla to the brightly-lit gas station across the street. Inside, I grabbed a Diet Coke and a single packet of aspirin before returning to my car.

Across the street lay the salty, weathered Raw Bar in all of its life-preserver-and-fake-crab-covered glory. I sipped at my soda greedily and felt the night's tension lighten and my headache disappear. Stowing the bright yellow packet in my pocket, I sat in my idling car and wondered why I hadn't stayed. Why hadn't I at least tried to make pleasant conversation and get to know her away from school? I'd never see her again anyway. What did I have to lose?

Finishing my soda, I returned to my old parking space and strode back into the Raw Bar confidently. At least I walked back in! I ordered a pitcher of light beer (I guessed that was what she would like) and with trembling hands, brought it and a clean glass over to Ms. Richard's table. She seemed surprised to see me, and my heart fluttered as she rose to greet me.

"Thanks for the offer," she replied as I hefted the sweaty pitcher of beer. "But maybe you and Cheryl can enjoy it. I was just leaving ... I've got this ... nasty headache."

Sure, it could have been a line, but she was rubbing her temples rather vigorously.

Just then, the crisp, yellow packet in my pocket called out to me, and I snatched it up, ripped it open and deposited two aspirin into her warm, soft hand.

Her eyes lit up and she swallowed them with a sip of fresh beer.

"Gee," she said with a smile she'd never revealed on the school grounds, "suddenly I feel a whole lot better!"

I've often looked back on that night in utter amazement. So many things seemed to align in just the right order. What if I'd gone to the right Raw Bar? What if I'd never bought that aspirin? What if I'd gone home instead of coming back? What if she had left before I got back? What if she preferred Tylenol?

Oh well, I guess I've had plenty of time to ponder those questions. Ms. Richard and I have been happily married for fifteen years.

Rusty Fischer lives in Florida, where he works full-time as a freelance writer. More than ever, he believes that Fate brought him and his lovely wife together—and keeps them together.

The Wig

By Brenda Warneka

Our hiking group met at Starbucks in Scottsdale at eight a.m. that Sunday. We were headed to Tonto National Forest for a hike in the Salome Creek Wilderness, northeast of Theodore Roosevelt Lake. Our hiking leader, Richard Allen, estimated it would take about two hours to get to the trailhead. We had twenty hikers and six vehicles. Some people double up and ride together when we go on our hiking trips. My husband, Dick, and I always drive alone so we can leave for home whenever we want to without inconveniencing anyone else.

It was a beautiful drive through the Arizona desert on a mid-March morning. With the recent rains, the sagebrush and other shrubs and grasses were green, and the spring wildflowers were beginning to bloom. Already a profusion of gold and purple flowers were showing off alongside the road, creeping out into the desert and chasing each other up the lower mountain slopes.

One of the places we drove past was the town of Punkin Center, where my former piano teacher had moved about twelve years before to live near her cousin, and I said to Dick that on the way back, I would like to stop and look her up, if it wasn't too late in the day. He asked, "How would you find her?"

I just *knew* I would, and answered confidently, "Oh, it would be easy because Punkin Center is so small, and her cousin owned a store there." Punkin Center, originally founded in 1945 as a weather station, is part of the Tonto Basin area.

I was having a mental block as I tried to remember my piano teacher's name. I wanted to say Eileen, but I knew that was wrong, and something like Thomas was coming to mind for her last name, but I knew that was wrong, too. I had never known her age, but she was fairly old, and always dressed up, with a too-large brown wig that reminded me of a beehive, slightly askew and falling over one eye, seemingly blocking her vision.

I remembered being very upset when she announced she was moving after I had taken piano lessons from her for several years. Not only was I quite fond of her, but I knew I would have trouble finding another piano teacher who would accommodate her schedule to my crazy work hours as a lawyer. And I was right. When she moved, it was basically the end of my piano instruction.

Now we left Route 85, a few miles before Roosevelt Lake, taking a dirt road cut-off that would lead us seventeen miles around the northern end of the lake to the trailhead. Just after we got off the main highway, we came to a large "Road Closed" barrier. We couldn't understand why there would be a road closure, and thought that perhaps someone had forgotten to remove the barrier, so we cautiously went around it. A short distance ahead, we saw what the problem was—the road crossed a wash, and the wash had water running through it at least two feet deep.

Some of the hikers wanted to drive on, but Richard Allen was concerned that even deeper water might lay ahead from recent rains. He suggested that we abandon our plans to hike to the Salome Creek Wilderness area and go to Four Peaks instead, another nearby wilderness area where we could take a hiking trail with which he was more familiar. When we got to the Four

Peaks area, we could see that the mountains still had snow in the upper elevations, so we agreed we would drive to the trailhead. If we ran into snow, we would just eat our lunches and head back home.

The dirt road to the Four Peaks trailhead was one lane, twisting and turning up the rugged mountain. Our vehicle hugged the inside of the mountain as Dick drove, while I looked off the steep cliff on my right to the desert foothills below. The rapid change in altitude was making me dizzy. Scared to death that our van would go off the side of this steep, narrow road, I suddenly insisted in a loud voice that I just couldn't take any more. After a particularly hair-raising bend, Dick stopped, managed to get the van turned around at a cut-out, and headed back down the mountain. When we got to a viewpoint where we could pull off and park, we ate our sandwiches and then left for home, stopping to buy gas along the highway.

As we came to Punkin Center, I said, "Let's stop and say hello to my teacher."

Realizing that I was serious, Dick pulled off the main highway to take the bypass through town, saying in a puzzled tone, "I don't know where to look." Since it was Sunday, the post office and most of the stores were closed, but as we were driving down the road through a hodgepodge of buildings, off to our left I saw a trading post up on a slight rise, set back maybe fifty yards from the road, just before a large embankment blocked my view. I said somewhat nonchalantly, "Oh, that must have been my teacher's cousin's store we just passed. I just spotted my piano teacher's wig."

Dick gave me an incredulous look and a "Huh?" but he backed up and pulled the van up the rise to the front of the store. I jumped out. Sure enough, it *was* my piano teacher, who had just closed the trading post for the day and was walking to her home, which was about sixty yards away.

She was extremely surprised, but immediately recognized us and invited us in to see her very nice manufactured house. She served us mango juice and cookies, and we got all caught up on what had happened in each other's lives in the years since she had moved from Phoenix. She had taught one of my sons piano, too, and I had the pleasure of telling her he was now married with two young children. As we visited, I finally remembered her name: Irene Thompson.

How I just *knew* that I would find Irene if we went to Punkin Center in search of her that day is a mystery. Fate took a sequence of synchronized steps to arrive at this harmonious outcome.

It was only because Irene had left the trading post exactly when she did, and we arrived there exactly when we did, that I saw her. If we had arrived a few minutes earlier, like if we hadn't stopped for gas on the highway, she still would have been inside the trading post when we drove by, and I honestly had no way of knowing the trading post was the store owned by her cousin until I saw Irene walking away from it. Just driving by, I would never have guessed it was even open on a Sunday as no cars were parked in front of it.

If we had driven by a few seconds later than we did, I would not have seen Irene because she already would have walked behind the embankment that blocked the view from the road, and a minute or two later, she would have been inside her house. Since I could not remember her name, there was no way I could have tried to locate her by asking any passersby if they knew her.

And I would not have realized that the woman I saw from the road, in the quick second before my view was blocked, was my teacher, either—except for the wig! You couldn't miss the wig! Irene did tell us she was ninety-one, and slightly hard of hearing, but otherwise seemed spry and doing fine.

When we got home, Dick sent Richard Allen an e-mail telling him what had happened to us. We received a reply the next morning that read:

Dear Dick and Brenda:

I'm glad things worked out OK for you. Actually, that bend was the worst place in the road. It got better after that. From the top, you can see Phoenix in the distance. I got the message that you had stopped. Thanks for being such good sports about all the changes of plans, etc. Nice that you could run into the teacher—maybe it was meant to be!

Richard

Yes, maybe it was meant to be. I can always go on another hike, but I never would have seen my piano teacher again if we had continued on our way to the Four Peaks trailhead. She passed away a couple of years later, and seeing her that day was indeed a pleasant, nostalgic experience for me.

As we go down the highway of life with incidents taking place, seemingly at random, "Fate" happens in a way we can't always explain.

The Seat in the Window

By Arlene Uslander

Fate is an unexpected external intrusion that brings out the strength or the weakness in me. I decide if I am too weak in disaster or to reassemble my life with divine contributions.

Garnet Hunt White

On the day I started my eighth month of pregnancy—a very difficult pregnancy that necessitated staying in bed most of the time—I was examined by my obstetrician, who gave me such a good report that my mother and I spent the afternoon picking out a layette. Tired from the shopping expedition, I lay down for a nap at my mother's house. When I woke up, I felt terrible pains in my abdomen, and as I stepped out of bed, saw that I was bleeding. My mother immediately called a taxi (it was before the days of 911) and took me to the hospital.

The baby, born by C-section, was a girl. I was told that she was perfect, but weighed only three pounds ("the size of a chicken," an insensitive neighbor remarked when she heard about the baby). I also was told that because she weighed so little, her chances of survival were only fifty-fifty. I couldn't see the baby yet because she was in an incubator, and I was too weak from my surgery and loss of blood to be wheeled to the nursery. I could only imagine what she looked like. My husband had seen her, and said she was beautiful.

During my second day in the hospital, my obstetrician told me the baby was "holding her own." That night, however, I awakened from a deep sleep and heard a nurse say something that sounded like "The Uslander baby." That was all I heard, but something in the tone of her voice made me suspect that what I had been dreading so much had happened.

The following morning, nurses flitted back and forth in my room. They all asked how I was feeling, but not one of them said a word to me about my baby. And I was afraid to ask. The phone, which had been ringing continuously the day before, was ominously silent. There was no sign of my doctor.

At eleven o'clock, my cousin's husband, Bob, an intern at the hospital, came into my room and pulled up a chair beside my bed. He took my hand and said, "I'm so sorry. She was a real fighter, but she was just too little to make it. Her tiny lungs gave out."

I didn't say a word, but from what he saw in my eyes, he realized that I hadn't been told. "Wasn't Dr. Reynolds in to see you?" he asked, an astonished look on his face.

I shook my head.

Bob took me in his arms and held me. My husband walked in crying. I couldn't cry. I just listened numbly as Bob and my husband angrily discussed the fact that my doctor had neglected to tell me that the baby had stopped breathing sometime around two a.m.

Nothing seemed real to me that day. Friends and relatives who had heard the news started calling to console me, and I spoke to them easily and rationally. I was still in shock. Thanks to a sleeping pill, I even slept through the night.

On the following day, the grief began to grip me like a shroud. Though in a private room, I was still on the maternity floor. Through the open door, I kept seeing nurses bringing babies to their mothers to be fed. When the closet door opened, I saw the brown maternity suit I had worn to the hospital. I couldn't bear to look at it. As the day wore on, I felt worse and worse. I kept visualizing the nursery my husband had painted pale yellow for the baby. I kept seeing the white baby furniture and the tiny little clothes my mother and I had picked out only a few days before.

During dinnertime, I was alone in my room. My husband had gone down to the cafeteria for a sandwich, and an orderly had left my dinner tray, which I hadn't touched. It was dark outside, and it seemed even darker inside. I started feeling very tense and agitated, as though all my nerves were standing on end. The idea of going home and seeing that empty nursery; spending days alone in the house (having given up my teaching job to be a full-time mother), and perhaps worst of all, the thought of becoming pregnant and possibly going through this terrible nightmare *again,* filled me with absolute panic. I kept staring at the partially open window, and I broke out in a cold, sickening sweat. The open window was beckoning me.

Suddenly, the door opened. A good-looking young man called me by name and asked if he could come in. I didn't recognize him at first. Then I realized who he was – a rabbi by the name of Richard Hirsch, who was a good friend of my father-in-law. I assumed that he had been sent on an official mission to talk to me about the death of my baby, but then he explained that his wife was in a room down the hall. She had given birth to a boy the day before. Richard had heard my name mentioned by someone visiting another patient, and he had inquired about me at the nurses' station.

Richard walked into my room and sat down on the window seat. "Are you cold?" he asked.

I nodded, and he reached up and closed the window. He stayed for about twenty minutes, telling me how sorry he was to hear about my baby. He said that his wife had lost two babies before finally giving birth to a beautiful, healthy baby boy.

He told me how thankful my husband and family must be that I was all right, because, apparently, my life had been in danger, too. And he assured me that time *would* ease the pain, and that and I would have another baby—perhaps many babies.

When Richard left, I suddenly felt much calmer. I finally cried—not so much for myself and my husband, or for my parents or my husband's parents, but for the tiny baby who had fought to stay alive, but "just couldn't make it." Something in Richard's eyes and voice ... in the soft, gentle touch of his hands on mine when he said goodbye ... finally allowed me to cry.

That was many years ago. I eventually gave birth to two wonderful sons, and now have four wonderful grandchildren. And yet, if not for that timely visit from the young rabbi, those sons and their children might not be here today.

Rabbi Richard Hirsch now lives in Israel. A friend recently told me that he was in town. "Do you remember him?" she asked me.

"Oh, yes," I said. "I remember him well." What I didn't tell her was that I will never forget how he sat down on the window seat in my hospital room and then closed the window. What I didn't tell her is that I have never gotten over the feeling that the young rabbi's appearance in my room *that night* was a case of more than someone just happening to be in the right place at the right time. I believe that Rabbi Hirsch was sent to be with me that night.

The Hand of Destiny

By Julia Macdonell

Coincidence is God's way of remaining anonymous.

Albert Einstein

When my Canadian husband died after thirty-one happily married years, I was trying to run a miniature farm outside the big city of San Paulo, Brazil. We also owned a small, one-bedroom apartment that we used when in the city.

Colin's estate was not very extensive, but he had willed it all to me since we had no children. It should have been a simple matter, but I needed a lawyer. A friend recommended one, and we started the legal work on the estate. I discovered later on that the lawyer I had chosen was going through a severe case of depression, and the proceedings took a long time. He had a young assistant who had just finished her training as a lawyer. She was twenty-seven, a tall, graceful woman named Katia, and he began to leave the case more and more in her hands.

Brazilian inheritance laws are complex. Parents and children are "necessary heirs." Colin was eighty-three when he died, but the judge insisted that I provide proof of his parents' deaths. His father had died when Colin was fourteen, and his mother when he was in his twenties. Colin had left his native town, Vancouver, British Columbia, forty years earlier, and I found nothing in his papers concerning his parents' deaths. His naturalization papers said he had no parents living, and our wedding certificate made it quite clear that they were deceased. But the judge insisted on death certificates, and it took Katia and me about six months before I was able to get Colin's sister-in-law and one of my cousins, then a resident in Vancouver, to search the cemeteries until they found the graves. They then provided a certificate that both Mr. and Mrs. Macdonell had, in fact, been buried there in Vancouver half a century before.

During this time, I grew to depend on Katia for emotional support, and one day, she introduced me to her mother, a small, very determined little person. A few weeks later, mother and daughter came to visit me in my apartment. The mother, Suzana, had given her apartment to Katia and her future husband, and they wanted to have it redecorated. Mother and daughter needed a place to live. Could they share my home with me until the wedding?

I agreed. I was lonely, and in any case, I spent most of my time out on the farm. The wedding took place ten months later, and I invited Suzana to go on living with me as long as she cared to. The young people could be on their own, although Suzana would still have a room at her old apartment.

So far, there was nothing unusual about a widow coming to share a home with her lawyer's mother. This could happen to anyone. But one day, at breakfast, Suzana and I were talking about my farm, and I commented on her understanding of my difficulties in running it.

"I ought to know something about country life. I was born on a farm and lived there until I was eight years old," she said.

"Where was it?" I asked.

"It was near Santa Cruz do Rio Pardo."

"That's curious. My uncle Alfred had a farm there. He was drowned in the Rio Pardo when I was nine, and his widow took her children back to England."

Suzana's eyes widened and she shivered. "Then it was the same farm. My father was overseer there, and I often heard the story about the former owner, an Englishman, who was drowned when his car slid off the river barge."

I shivered, too. I had troubled memories of Auntie Ruth staying in our home before she returned to England to raise five children on her own.

There are twelve million people in Sao Paulo, and tens of thousands of lawyers. Suzana and I still share the same apartment and all of life's ups and downs. We feel we were destined to meet.

Julia Macdonell is a second-generation Brazilian whose British and American grandparents came to Brazil in the late nineteenth century. She grew up in a bilingual home and attended an American grade school and high school. She worked as a bilingual secretary-translator and, for fifteen years, taught English in an accredited language school. She is an avid student of Brazilian history and folklore, and in recent years, following a childhood dream, is taking writing courses and participating in writers' groups. She wishes to record both the legends of the countryside and the experiences of a lifetime. Her novel, *The Boy and the Warrior*, was published by e-Press Online in July 2008.

.

What Is Fate?

Fate happens to me on a regular basis. I need something, and it happens. I think of someone, and they call. I pride myself on what others see as simply a coincidence. To me, it is a sign that I am on the true path to my authentic self and that I am living my destiny. I strive to make fate my reality, and life is a quiet thing.

Amy Casey
Actress, singer

THE MYSTERY OF FATE:

Taxi Driver's Passenger

A taxi driver found the son he had last seen thirty-four years ago as a fare in the back of his cab. The chance reunion came when Barry Bagshaw, sixty-one, picked up a fare at a motel near Brighton in southern England. A short time into the journey, the woman accompanying the man in the back spotted the driver's identity badge and noticed he had the same surname as her boyfriend.

"The blood just drained out of me when he said 'I'm your son,'" Barry told BBC radio. "I didn't recognize him at first. It certainly won't be another thirty-four years before I see him again."

His son Colin, a thirty-nine-year-old chef, was about to leave the area for good, believing his father was dead, even though they found they lived just streets apart.

Barry, who has another son and a daughter, lost touch with his children when his marriage broke down while he was serving in the army in Hong Kong.

The Emissary

By Siegfried Brian Barger

Fate is an unexpected intervention by the Divine that often is considered to be coincidence by mere mortals like us.

My sister was dying of cancer. I was very sad over her illness, but I had only to think of the constant anguish suffered by my parents, who were caring for her, to feel even sadder. "Get your affairs in order," the doctors had bluntly told her. "There is nothing that can be done. Maybe you have six months; maybe not." But my family does not dissuade easily. My father, who was a cross between an ill-tempered grizzly and a lovable koala, began to assemble the considerable financial resources necessary to pay for an experimental bone marrow transplant. In 1990, when this happened, such a procedure was considered miraculous if it allowed a patient to survive more than a year or so.

One afternoon, I found myself in an uncomfortable social setting. I did not know most of the people who were there. The topic that occupied our conversation was personal tragedy. *Great,* I thought. *Just the thing to cheer me up.*

A young woman was leading the conversation. She looked vaguely familiar, but I certainly did not know her. Lanky and slightly awkward, she was the kind of utterly common girl who would normally escape one's notice. Even her name was extraordinarily commonplace: Mary. As she spoke, though, it was obvious that there was something unusual about her. She'd had a dream, she said; a very young baby was critically ill and the child's doctors had used all the medical magic they could muster. It was just a matter of time. The dream was so real, she told us that it consumed her thoughts. She could see every feature of the baby—her face, her smile, the details of the yellow dress she wore. Mary said she was convinced a real baby existed—this baby—who was somewhere dying, and she could not ignore the dream any longer. She called a network of her friends and told them of her dream, and she insisted they had to pray for the baby. And so they did.

Some weeks later, Mary continued, an old friend invited her to see her new home. The two women had not seen each other for years. When she arrived, her friend radiated delight and happiness. There was the new home of which she was so proud, but mostly she had a surprise for Mary, and that was the real reason behind the invitation. The surprise: to show Mary her new baby girl. "We call her our 'Miracle Baby,'" the mother glowed, handing her to Mary. "The doctors had told us she would die; but she did not." Suddenly, Mary realized why her dream had been so powerful and her need to pray so intense: This was the sick baby of her dream—the Miracle Baby—now in her arms, wearing her new yellow Easter dress.

As we all began to leave our gathering later that afternoon, I looked for Mary. I needed her help for my sister. We spoke only for a few moments that afternoon.

"My sister is terminal," I said. "I need your prayers, and the prayers of your friends." I could barely talk. A huge knot of emotion sat in my throat, and tears welled in my eyes. Yes, she said, very matter-of-factly, they would be happy to pray for her.

I felt a bit foolish. I had, after all, approached a perfect stranger and asked for a miracle, practically blubbering on my double-breasted suit in the process. A crazy continuum of feelings wandered through me as she walked away that afternoon: gullibility, relief, hope, stupidity. In the ensuing weeks, I looked for her at some of the places I thought she might frequent, but nothing.

Then as I was walking to a little delicatessen one day, Mary happened to see me coming down the street. She called me over.

"Oh, listen, I'm glad I found you," she said, seemingly short of time. "Tell your sister a lot of us prayed for her. She's going to be fine. Her cancer is gone."

That was it. No big explanation of how she knew this.

Her cancer is gone.

Then she offered a little wave and departed as though we were old friends.

Eleven years have passed since that afternoon. To her doctors' amazement, my sister is alive today, and cancer free. She is not perfect; the bone marrow transplant left her with anemia, a compromised immune system and unrelenting fatigue, but she is alive and happy.

I am sure that most who hear this story will conclude that nothing more than coincidence was at work here. The transplant worked. Period. That is what they would say. But, that is an over-simplification of our world. Virtually all of the other women my sister met in the bone marrow unit that winter died long ago. She is one of just two survivors.

And Mary? I have not seen her since that casual meeting on the street more than a decade ago. To be honest, I doubt that I would even recognize her. She was, after all, just a normal, lanky, awkward girl. A curious emissary of Fate.

Siegfried Brian Barger lives in Tucson, Arizona, where he works in advertising. He is the author of *Fontana* - a novel that people who love animals, and have a warm spot in their hearts for the older generation, will find particularly heartwarming. He is currently working on a sequel.

Hebrew Folk Tale

Anonymous

King Solomon's servant ran breathlessly into the court. "Please! Let me borrow your fastest horse!" he said to the king. "I must be in a town ten miles south of here by nightfall!"

"Why?" asked King Solomon.

"Because," said his shuddering servant, "I just met Death in the garden! Death looked me in the face! I know for certain I'm to be taken, and I don't want to be around when Death comes to claim me."

"Very well," said the king. "My fastest horse has hooves like wings. Take him." Then Solomon walked into the garden. He saw Death sitting there with a perplexed look on its face. "What's wrong?" asked King Solomon.

Death replied, "Tonight I'm supposed to claim the life of your servant whom I just now saw in your garden, but I'm supposed to claim him in a town ten miles south of here! Unless he has a horse with hooves like wings, I don't see how he could get there by nightfall."

The Wave

By Mark S. Daniels

Fate: forces that route your life on the proper course, from beginning to end. Life's ebb and flow and your place in it.

Skywriters. I used to watch them as a child.

High over my home in the San Fernando Valley, during the early 1960s, flying the old two-winged "biplanes" from an era now long gone, making magic against the vast blue, heavenly slate. Using their aircraft as though a pen; creating those enormous, puffed-white letters of an alphabet I had yet to learn. Craftsmen in the sky, making larger than life those huge, spacey messages, seemingly so trivial today. I watched them so long ago, floating across the apparent stillness of those crystal-blue California skies. "Scripture" they were, these banners driven slowly across the valley heights by winds aloft, delivering "commandments" and "messages," seemingly from God:

DRINK COCA COLA
4TH OF JULY AT PACIFIC OCEAN PARK
L.A. COUNTY FAIR, OCT. 1-31, POMONA FAIRGROUNDS

In sunny California, that's how one would note the season's change. The summers seemed to last forever, and so we'd drink our Coca Cola on the drive down to the beach, following Santa Monica Boulevard and the like-minded in their automobiles, who bottle-necked us at every stoplight for what seemed like a hundred miles. We might stop at the Will Rogers Estate on the way to the beach and look at the old house, or the grass polo fields where Wiley Post used to land his famous wooden airplane, the "Winnie May," long ago retired as an exhibit to a museum known as the "Smithsonian."

Then we'd head to Will Rogers State Beach.

Boy, people sure liked Will Rogers!

"Hey, Ma! Who's Will Rogers?"

And then my brother Mike, my sister Chris, and I, we'd jump and dance in the surf, picnic with Mom on the beach, walk the shore at the water's edge, look for seashells in the foam, and try to recite stupid things like "Sally sells seashells at the seashore!" God only knows why, other than to laugh ourselves silly while trying to outdo each other with our grand recitals.

Then we'd explore the barnacle-covered rocks beyond the water's edge, looking for starfish, sea anemones and octopi that would cling there in the waters of Santa Monica Bay … in a day when those waters were still clean.

Then Mom, her gentleman friend (since Dad had "up and split"), and I would hang around in that warm, mellow evening breeze, beside that gentle bay that was friend to us all. A bay upon which stood two timeless wooden structures: the first, that massive, towering keeper of the rocket sled on wheels, the roller-coaster-laden Pacific Ocean Park pier; the second, the trendy yet nostalgic antiquity at the end of Route 66, the Santa Monica Pier, where the merry-go-round forever twirled and the calliope music played; a tiny corner of my world where there was laughter under the stars.

That was back in a time when "Ike" was our president, when the summers were never ending, and life was good. These were among my first memories.

As was the summer I nearly drowned. The year was 1959, and I was three-and-a-half-years old. My brother, sister, and I were walking at the edge of the surf at Santa Monica Beach, looking for seashells. As usual, we were letting the waves roll across our bare feet as the tide caressed the shoreline. The three of us liked the feeling of motion we got when the surf returned to the sea—somewhat of a sinking feeling that seemed to drag you with it.

Mom had given us all the warnings, such as not swimming for twenty minutes after eating or we'd get cramps and drown.

"Ma? What are 'gramps'?"

She, of course, warned us of the dreaded "Rip Tide." Personally, I thought he was a character from Grandma's favorite song, "Mack the Knife," or perhaps a famous actor.

In actuality, the riptide was a strong underwater current known as the "undertow" that exists when nearby storms of great strength create a hydraulic force that builds a sandbar near the shore. As the sandbar grows, the water in between builds up until it overflows the barrier, then cuts a path back out to sea. Working through physics, as though a venturi tube, the pool of water passes through the channel, increasing velocity at the narrow point, before exiting the sandbar in a rush. A "ripping" is thus created—like a saw blade clearing through a piece of wood, becoming a device that can drag at first, then flow quickly, ultimately taking even the best swimmers out to sea very rapidly.

As it was, I didn't know how to swim. I hadn't wandered far from our mother when a wave came in, and I ran out to chase it back to sea. A big mistake, because the wave was followed by a second, larger wave, before the first had even retreated. That larger wave grabbed me like fingers curling on a hand, and proceeded to pull me right in.

The sensation of being tumbled in the sand, under the water, was as heavenly as it was frightening. I couldn't breathe; I was swallowing great amounts of water, and I could see my sister and brother trying to grab me from the sea without being pulled in themselves. In fact, they were chasing me as the wave took me out towards the ocean. Neither could catch up. My ears, immersed in water, could hear only the pouring, bubbling sound of the surf, and an occasional word or two my sister yelled to me through the brine.

I was running out of air and becoming weaker. I was scared, and yet the feeling was of being so airy and light. There was no feeling of suffocation; I would liken it to being in the womb, though I am hard-pressed to remember that far back. Just the same, I do think that was the closest I ever came to being in the hands of something angelic, though I did not see an angel.

Or did I?

I remember looking directly at my sister, and the effect was as though looking through a plate glass window with a waterfall rushing over it, and there she was—my big sister—desperately reaching out for me.

"Grab my hand!" she yelled

I couldn't reach her. I was too weak. I made one last thrust, and she caught my hand, clenched it, and pulled with all her might, dragging me from the wave. One hand trying to take me out to sea, the other trying to pull me back in to shore, and the smaller of the two hands won!

The reality of my situation was clear as I gagged and spat up saltwater, then began crying, my lungs once again filling with air. No doctor around, but I should have been slapped on the back.

My brother and my sister were laughing even though they were scared to death.

"We almost lost you!" my sister said. "You almost died!"

Fifty years later, I still haven't learned how to swim. Go figure. I still love the water's edge, and I want to spend time on the open waters of the Pacific. Wherever I can find an ocean, a lake, a river, or even a stream, somehow, I can find peace there.

Only my Creator knows why.

Mark S. "Bear" Daniels is a professional writer and photographer who manages *Images of Light Internet Press Service* at www.ilips.net. Daniels has been published by *United Press International* (UPI), *Associated Press* (AP), *Reuters* and others. While working as a photographer for *United Press International*, Daniels became only the second FAA-sanctioned photographer in the history of air racing to ride in an Unlimited Class racer during an actual air race competition. He is father to Christine Carol Daniels and Ida Renee Daniels, and the proud grandfather of Cody Allen Newton.

Fascination: A Message from Beyond?

By Arlene Uslander

It would have been my mother's ninetieth birthday. She had died two years before. My mother was born and raised in the Bronx, New York. Her name was Lillian, and she often referred to herself as "Lily from the Bronx."

One of her favorite songs was "Fascination," as popularized by singer Jane Morgan. The reason is because she and my father were invited to a very elegant party at the Pump Room, which was Chicago's classiest restaurant in the fifties, and the most memorable part of the evening for her was the fact that there was a violinist stationed at the bottom of a long, winding staircase that led up to the ladies' room, and he was playing "Fascination" when she came down. Whenever my mother heard that song after that evening, especially in her later years after my father had died, it reminded her of being with him at that lovely party during a wonderful time of her life.

I left for work in my car that morning thinking of my mother, thinking of her a lot, as I always do, but especially because it was her birthday. My car radio had not worked for many months. Any time I turned it on, there was nothing but static. I had thought about having it fixed, but the car was old, and it would have cost a lot to fix or replace the radio, so I figured that I could do without it until I got a new car. I often took my battery-operated cassette player with me and listened to tapes in the car, but not on this particular morning.

Just out of force of habit, I turned on the radio. As usual, there was nothing but static, so I turned it off. About ten minutes later, I decided to give it another try, though I really don't know why.

Lo and behold, it worked! A song was playing. There was no static. It was clear as a bell. And what was the song? "Fascination."

Well, that sort of gave me chills. Forget the "sort of." It *did* give me chills. Even more eerie was the fact that soon after the song ended, so did the radio. It stopped working again. This time for good!

As soon as I arrived at my office, I told my co-workers about "Fascination," and they agreed that it was strange. Very strange. I sat down at my desk and took a look at my day-to-day desk calendar, which advertises a different website each day, and the first word that caught my eye was *BRONX*. The ad said: "The Bronx is up and the Battery is down!"—or maybe it was vice versa—advertising a restaurant guide for New York City. The fact that this particular advertisement appeared on my desk calendar the day of my mother's birthday blew my mind. It was almost like I was getting some kind of message, and I didn't usually believe in that sort of thing.

That was last year. This year, on my mother's birthday, the day was almost over, and there had been no sign. Then, just before I went to bed, I sat down at my computer to check my e-mail. I am a freelance editor, and there was a letter from a man telling me that he needed someone to help him get two manuscripts ready for publication. The first one was called "Grandpa and Lily," the second was "Lily's Walk to the Moon."

I try especially hard to be on my best behavior all day, the day of my mother's birthday, just in case *someone* is watching me …

Fate magazine, 2003. All rights reserved. Used with permission.

What is Fate?

The problem of synchronicity has puzzled me for a long time, ever since the middle twenties, when I was investigating the phenomena of the collective unconscious and kept on coming across connections which I simply could not explain as chance groupings or "runs."[1] What I found were "coincidences" which were connected so meaningfully that their "chance" concurrence would represent a degree of improbability that would have to be expressed by an astronomical figure.

Carl Jung, *Collected Works Vol. 8*

THE MYSTERY OF FATE:

Dispatched

By Susan Lynn Kingsbury

The following is a true story of fate. Names have been changed to protect those involved. A friend of mine, a police officer, shared his story with me. Read on to find out how two men find themselves in the wrong place at the wrong time.

November 1992

After a one-year assignment in the Detective Bureau, Officer Tom Howard, a veteran of many years with the police department, found himself back on the streets, working as a training officer. A rookie officer rode with him for the first part of his shift. Howard worked shift two, from noon to ten p.m., and the rookie's training officer wasn't on duty, so rather than have him sit around at the front counter doing nothing, Howard took the rookie with him for the first part of his scheduled duty.

At around five p.m., he dropped the rookie off at the station and went back out on patrol as a solo unit. It had been dark about an hour when he was dispatched to a silent burglary alarm covering the back door of a health food store.

Sounds from the police radio broke the silence in the patrol car.

"David 2. 459 silent at 1098 North Main Street. Griswell's Health Foods. Cover the back door."

"David 2, copy." Howard wrote down the address in his steno pad. *Not much has changed,* he thought. He remembered going out on calls to that same store when he was on patrol before. The neighborhood knuckleheads had a habit of kicking in the back door to break in. Heading in that direction, he began thinking of the layout of the store, and a plan of action for when he got there. He knew better than to approach the call as routine. It didn't matter how many false alarms the dispatch unit received; the next one could be the real thing.

"David 2, 10-97." He let Dispatch know he'd arrived on the scene.

"David 2, 10-4. Advise on backup."

Pulling into the dirt lot adjacent to the south side of the store, he eased the nose of the car close to the corrugated fence which separated the two lots, then got out. He walked to the front of the car and stepped onto the front bumper so he could look over the six-foot-plus fence and get a view of the back door of the store. It stood wide open.

"I've got an open rear door. Send a backing unit," he told Dispatch.

"David 2, copy."

Walking east to an area where it was easier to climb over the fence, he hurtled over into the back lot behind the health food store. On the other side, he found himself behind a couple of rows of ice cream trucks that blocked his view of the store. Moving forward a few steps, he peered between two trucks and spotted a man coming out the open door. A bright light over the rear entrance shone down on him.

The man, who appeared to be in his late forties, wore a pair of black slacks and a white dress shirt open at the neck, with his sleeves rolled up. His right hand gripped the butt of a gun he held in front of him.

Howard pointed his flashlight in the man's direction and yelled "Stop! Police! Put the gun down!"

The man looked at Howard and hesitated, but said nothing. Then he walked toward an older black Lincoln sedan that was parked near an old dilapidated building at the back of the property. He never took his eyes off Howard.

Very unusual behavior. Why doesn't he answer? Howard thought.

By now the man had moved within fifteen to twenty feet of him.

Howard yelled out again "Stop! Police! Put the gun down!"

Nothing.

A silhouette of a second man appeared from inside the rear entrance of the store. He had not yet stepped out into the light over the doorway, and Howard couldn't make out any details of his appearance.

Great, now there are two of them. How many more are inside? he wondered.

The silhouetted man quickly went back into the building. The white-shirted one with the gun momentarily turned his back to Howard. He then turned around and took a small step toward him. Gripping the gun in both hands, he raised it up, pointed, and shot one round. Howard was hit in the chest and the impact through his Kevlar vest knocked him back against one of the trucks. He shot two rounds at the man as he fell, but the bullets missed his target.

Righting himself, Howard found a spot behind another truck to take cover. He positioned himself so he could contain the shooter and watch him more easily. Then he let Dispatch know about the shots fired.

He yelled again, "Police! Put the gun down!"

Howard felt a burning sensation in his upper chest. Something sharp poked him. Reaching his hand up, he undid his uniform shirt and looked at his Kevlar vest. A dime-sized jagged hole showed through the corner of the choke plate (a thin metal plate that slides into the vest and covers the middle of the chest). His T-shirt and vest had blood on them. The bulletproof vest had stopped the bullet, but the sharp edges of the damaged plate cut into his skin.

Exhaustion overtook him. *When will this nightmare end? When will he stop shooting at me?*

By now the man was standing up on the porch of the old dilapidated building at the back of the property. He shot two more rounds at Howard.

Returning fire, the policeman realized that he had somehow hit his target. He watched as the man took a few hesitant steps back from the doorway and collapsed in a heap.

Sirens whined in the distance. Howard heard officers calling out that they had arrived at the scene.

"In the back of the store," he advised over the radio. Still, none of the back-ups appeared. *Why is it taking so long for them to get here?* He knew he was in bad shape from the blunt trauma of the bullet to his vest.

"We're at the entrance of the building," he heard the response, and seconds later, two officers came barreling through a gate into the backyard.

The two officers checked on Howard, and after he gave them a fast update they moved forward as he stumbled back through the open gate, telling Dispatch "I'm retreating."

The paramedics were waiting in the dirt lot near his black and white. They put him on a stretcher and cut his shirt off to get at his wound. One of the officers on the scene, Officer Jones, stayed while they worked on Howard.

Later, Jones got quiet, and Howard asked, "What's going on?"

"He's dead," Jones said

"The man tried to kill me. He had every opportunity to leave, but instead, he started shooting at me."

"He was the store owner's brother."

"What? He never said a word. All he did was look at me." Howard paused. "Why didn't he say anything? Why did he shoot at me?"

The local newspaper told the whole story the next day.

At seven p.m. the previous night, Officer Tom Howard was dispatched and responded to a silent burglary alarm at a health food store, but had gone to the wrong location. As a result, he ended up at an ice cream business. He was engaged in a horrific shootout and was hit in the chest. His Kevlar vest stopped the bullet and saved his life.

The report went on to say that the store owner's brother was not as lucky. He came out of the rear of the store carrying a nine-millimeter handgun. Despite Officer Howard's continual demands to put the gun down, the man proceeded to open fire on the officer. Howard returned fire, and the store owner's brother died at the scene.

According to the newspaper article, no one knew why the man opened fire on Officer Howard, but because the ice cream business owner and his brother were from the Middle East, speculation was that they didn't understand what Howard had said and thought they were being robbed. The irony of the tragedy was that the dispatched call was for Griswell's Health Foods' new location; the business had moved from the old location only two months before. And, the alarm from the health food store's new location that evening was false.

Both men would have been better off being somewhere else that night. Even though Dispatch had put out the burglary call for the new address, and Howard had written it down correctly, he responded to the old address from force of habit. The manager and his brother, according to what police found out later, were on their way to put the day's earnings and receipts into a safe in the dilapidated building at the back of the property.

Much later, Howard discovered that the man who shot at him had been a police lieutenant in his native country. What were the odds of two police officers, from different countries, having a shootout? What were the chances that a bullet fired from Howard's gun would ricochet off the vinyl-covered hard top of the black Lincoln and into the center of the man's back at the exact moment he turned to enter the building?

What would have happened if Howard had had the rookie with him? He assumes they would have ended up at the correct address. Or would the rookie have been involved in the tragedy, too?

Howard spent some time in the hospital. The black and blue bruising that covered his chest was a telltale sign of the amount of impact the bulletproof vest had taken.

Four days after the shooting, the dead man's family filed a wrongful death suit in federal court. During the trial, affirmed in the appeal that followed, the jury found that Howard had not been negligent, even though he had gone to the wrong location.

Ten Years Later

Today, Officer Tom Howard still feels guilt over the whole ugly incident. So many questions remain unanswered. Why did force of habit send him to the wrong address? Why did the man shoot at him? Howard has spent many sleepless nights wondering about the shooting, and the only answer he can come up with is that the gunman didn't believe he was a police officer.

"He must have thought I'd come to steal his money," he reflects. "Maybe he couldn't see me clearly."

Howard may never know the answers to his questions, and he may never have closure.

He says, "It's not like on television and in the movies. I was involved in a gun battle, was shot and lived. I killed a man. It wasn't glamorous."

Susan Lynn Kingsbury is both a fiction and nonfiction author whose articles, book reviews, essays and columns are published in numerous magazines and newsletters, including *Cruising World, Latitudes and Attitudes, Good Old Boat, The Ensign, Writing Etc.* and the *NAWW Writer's Guide.* Her mystery short story, "Waiting is Murder," is included in the anthology *Little Sisters, Volume 1,* released in 2007. Susan's current projects include a private eye mystery, a police crime novel, and a nonfiction book about sailing.

She also enjoys speaking, moderating and participating as a panel member for Sisters in Crime and Elderhostel Life Long Learning, as well as in other writing and education venues.

You can find her at *hometown.aol.com/WritingsbySiLK.*

Fawn's Choice

By Colleen Kay Behrendt

It had been a little over a year since our dog Rex had passed away at the ripe old age of seventeen. We were fortunate to have had him with us that long. We weren't sure we wanted to get another dog, become attached, and then go through the painful, but inevitable, process of losing a beloved pet again. However, we finally decided that our household was not complete; it was time to get another dog. Although we had seen several dogs that we had warmed up to right away at an animal shelter, my husband, Dennis, was not interested. He said we should get a Great Dane who had "been mistreated and really needed a good home."

"Honey, what are the chances of our getting a dog with such specific requirements—a Great Dane who has been mistreated?" I asked. "Pretty slim, don't you think?"

"Well, we have to try," he said. "That really is the kind of dog I think we should get."

We didn't talk about it anymore.

On our way home from a Las Vegas vacation to Yuma, Arizona, where we live part of the year, we stayed overnight at a motel in Prescott. The next morning, Dennis went to the motel restaurant to have coffee; I remained in the room. I turned on television, something that I rarely do that early in the day. The program was "Pets on Parade," sponsored by the Arizona Humane Society, showing animals that were available for adoption.

Near the end of the show, a Humane Society representative said, "We have one more dog who will be at our special adoption tomorrow, but we could not bring her today. She has just been spayed and is recovering from the surgery. This dog will need someone who can handle a very large dog and also be able to administer medication and meet the needs of her special diet." This really piqued my curiosity. (I later found out that the "special diet" consisted of feeding the dog small meals three times a day, and in addition to her dog food, she would need to be fed home-cooked items, such as eggs and vegetables. It was a lot more complicated than just pouring food from a bag or a can into a bowl.)

At that moment, a picture of the dog appeared on the television screen. I could hardly believe my eyes. It was a Great Dane! Her name was Fawn. Was this a coincidence or what? Could this be the dog Dennis had been talking about?

The picture of Fawn was pathetic. She was so skinny and sad looking. The announcer then said that Fawn was two years old and was recovering from starvation and beatings.

I started to cry, and said out loud, "Fawn, we will come and get you tomorrow."

Just as the program went off the air, Dennis walked into the room. He took one look at me and asked "What's wrong? Why are you crying?"

"Honey, remember the Great Dane you were talking about?" I said. "Well, I know where she is."

"What are you talking about?" he asked.

I told him about the program I had seen on TV. Dennis was overwhelmed. I asked him, "Did you have a dream about a dog like that? What made you say that you wanted a Great Dane who had been mistreated?"

"No, I didn't have a dream. I just thought about the fact that there are dogs who have been mistreated and need good homes. I figured we would look for one who really needs us."

"But why did you say it should be a Great Dane?" I asked.

"I don't know; maybe because Rex was part Great Dane, and he was such a wonderful dog."

We called the Arizona Humane Society to find out more about Fawn. The only thing we were told was that this was a special case, and that if we were interested in adopting Fawn, we would have to go through an investigation, which would include giving our social security numbers and references. It sounded like a criminal background check. Also, the Humane Society would check with our veterinarian regarding our ability to care for a large animal with health problems. Not unlike what people go through when they want to adopt a baby. We gave them the necessary information.

We were told that there had been many calls about Fawn after the broadcast, and that if there were several interested parties present at the adoption, a drawing would take place. The winner would then be checked out to see if he or she qualified to adopt her.

On Sunday morning we drove to the Humane Society. The adoption program was to begin at one o'clock. The hour-and-a-half drive from Prescott to Phoenix seemed endless as the minutes slowly ticked away.

Fawn was the last animal to be put up for adoption. There were about twenty people interested in her. Many of them left when they saw how pathetic the dog looked. A Humane Society officer paraded Fawn around the group. She stopped by Dennis. The officer tried to pull her away, but she sat down and would not move. It was as if she were saying "This is who I pick!"

Through a process of elimination by the Humane Society officers, the final count was down to six. Dennis was in this group. The officers handed out numbered tickets, putting the matching stubs in a box. The officer then had a person from the audience draw the winning ticket stub.

The officer read the winning number. Dennis yelled, "That's my number!" Then he stooped down and hugged Fawn, who was still at his side. She gave him a great, big, sloppy kiss.

The officer took Dennis's ticket to make sure the numbers matched. They did. He then shook Dennis's hand and said, "Congratulations, it looks like this is a perfect match. Fawn certainly likes you, and I can see that the feeling is mutual. And by the way, we already did our investigation. Take Fawn home."

Was this really a coincidence? Why did Dennis mention a Great Dane as being the breed of dog we would take in? Why did I turn on the TV that particular morning, and why was it tuned to "Pets on Parade"? Was this fate after all?

Colleen Kay Behrendt lives with her husband and their beloved canine companion. She has two adult daughters and one stepdaughter who have blessed her with seven grandchildren. During the summer, Colleen and her husband reside in northeastern Minnesota, and during the winter, in southwestern Arizona. Colleen considers herself fortunate to be able to live in what she considers the best of both climates, as well as two of the prettiest regions of the United States. She is a member of the Desert Writer's Club in Wellton, Arizona. Her other interests are traveling, fishing, reading, animals, learning all she can about computer skills, knitting and crocheting.

Earthshakes

By Jerry Bower

It was January 17, 1994. Depending on what a person happened to be doing, or where they happened to be, the earth moved in two very distinct directions that day.

If you were my wife on that morning in 1994, and just happened to sit down to play a few quarters in a progressive slot machine in the back lobby of the Golden Nugget Casino in downtown Las Vegas, you would have been in for a very pleasant surprise.

But let's change the venue for a moment. Suppose that instead of being in a casino in Las Vegas, you were driving on a freeway in Los Angeles at a certain time in the morning. If that were the case, you would be in for a very different surprise.

In Las Vegas, for my wife, the earth shook in a minor way when three of the same symbols lined up in the right position of a slot machine in the lobby of the Golden Nugget Casino, and she instantly won twelve thousand dollars.

That same morning in Los Angeles, some other individual had a very different appointment with fate when maybe on the way to work, the earth shook in a very real way, and the freeway, heaving from a massive earthquake, parted in a wide gap. The overpass in front of that driver, which a few seconds before had to have been as firm as rock to handle all the traffic it did, suddenly disappeared, collapsing onto the highway below it. And that individual, driving his or her car, went catapulting into midair where the overpass had been.

Two people, on the same day, in two different places, had their lives change, either for better or worse, because the earth shook at a precise time.

You ask, "What's the point?"

Let me explain. The following year, 1995, my wife and I were at the same convention in Las Vegas that we had been at the year before when she had hit the jackpot. On the morning of January 17, in the main casino at Bally's on the Strip, after eating a leisurely breakfast, my wife stopped to play a roll of quarters in a progressive slot machine. A few pulls later, four symbols lined up in the right sequence, and she won over $475,000. Weird, isn't it? Two mind-boggling wins in two successive years, *on the same day of the year,* defying unimaginable odds, to garner close to half a million dollars. But wait, that's only part of it.

On that same day in 1995, again the earth shook twice: a minor tremor in Las Vegas, where my wife hit her second jackpot, and another full-fledged quake in Kobe, Japan, where many people either lost their lives or had their lives changed forever. Now, after the glow of the past excitement has worn off, I often think back on both of those days with mixed emotions, recalling the rush of elation and disbelief at defying the Las Vegas odds twice. I think about the revelry, telling our friends, who were there with us at the same convention, about our good fortune. And my wife calling our kids back home, who, after the first announcement of the winnings, wouldn't believe her. I recall the lavish celebrations afterwards on the Las Vegas Strip, recounting the events of a lifetime with any stranger who would listen.

And after that—after the formal celebration—our own personal celebration back at our hotel room, into the small hours of the morning. Then the two of us, lying there satisfied and comfortable in our bed, falling asleep close to each other, surrounded by the luxury of our hotel room, never once thinking about all of the other lives that had been changed in so many different ways on those two unbelievable days.

Fate runs in streaks, both good and bad, sometimes confusing us in a hodgepodge of seemingly unrelated happenings, though always driving toward some destination reserved for all of us, its unsuspecting subjects. I truly believe that Fate knows no boundaries. It works indiscriminately, demonstrating its control over everyone.

Jerry Bower is a retired farmer from Shiawassee County, Michigan, who considers himself a "modern-day adventurer." He loves to fish, hunt and explore, seeking out places where he can no longer see utility poles, concrete, or other humans. He is the author of many short stories and is presently working on his first novel. His works have been published in *Outdoor Life* and *Woods* and *Water News.* His favorite quote is an old Indian saying: "If one sits still long enough, the trees will speak and the dead will come visit." He thinks he may be looking for that place where it is possible for him to stay put long enough.

Epilogue

One of the things we hope you will take away from this book is the reassurance of how often things go right when they could have gone wrong, and how often there is no explanation for the interplay of events that exist to make whatever happens happen, except Fate or a Higher Power. Of course, the stories in this book often involve matters of life and death, and the good is inextricably interwoven with the bad, but living life successfully requires that we be philosophical and dwell on the positive aspects of things that happen.

We hope that you, the reader, will identify with that. A central theme that comes through to us in many of the stories is the survival of the human spirit in the face of adversity. Another theme we hope you became aware of as you read this book is the willingness of people to risk their lives to help others.

We believe that Fate is present in everyone's lives, but we also think there are some individuals who are more intuitive, or more in tune with what is going on in their surroundings and relationships, and thus more prone to recognize the part that Fate, or a Higher Power, plays in their lives.

We hope that you think about the role of Fate or that Higher Power in your own life as a result of reading this book. We also hope that reading these true, inspirational stories, which people from all over the world and all walks of life were kind enough to share with us, caused you to give serious thought to the question: "Was it just a common coincidence, or was it Divine Intervention?

The Editors

4827265R0

Made in the USA
Charleston, SC
22 March 2010